D0855764

Midcentury Christmas

Midcentury Christmas

Holiday Fads, Fancies, and Fun from 1945 to 1970

 BY **SARAH ARCHER**

THE COUNTRYMAN PRESS
A DIVISION OF W. W. NORTON & COMPANY
INDEPENDENT PUBLISHERS SINCE 1923

Copyright © 2016 by Sarah Archer

All rights reserved
Printed in the United States of America

For information about permission to reproduce
selections from this book, write to Permissions,
The Countryman Press, 500 Fifth Avenue,
New York, NY 10110

For information about special discounts for bulk purchases,
please contact W. W. Norton
Special Sales at specialsales@wwnorton.com or
800-233-4830

Manufacturing by Versa Press
Book design by LeAnna Weller Smith
Production manager: Devon Zahn

Library of Congress Cataloging-in-Publication Data

Names: Archer, Sarah, author.
Title: Midcentury Christmas : holiday fads, fancies, and fun
    from 1945 to 1970 / Sarah Archer.
Description: New York : The Countryman Press, 2016. |
    Includes bibliographical references
    and index.
Identifiers: LCCN 2016029688 | ISBN 9781581574029 (hard-
    cover : alk. paper)
Subjects: LCSH: Christmas—United States—
    History—20th century.
Classification: LCC GT4986.A1 A73 2016 | DDC 394.2663—
    dc23 LC record available at https://lccn.loc.
    gov/2016029688

The Countryman Press
www.countrymanpress.com

A division of W. W. Norton & Company, Inc.
500 Fifth Avenue, New York, NY 10110
www.wwnorton.com

10 9 8 7 6 5 4 3 2 1

Opposite: Pyrex Christmas Party Mug, Corning Glass
Works, Charleroi, 1963. Collection of The Corning
Museum of Glass, Corning, New York.

For my mother, who has the same
handwriting as Santa Claus

CONTENTS

INTRODUCTION 9

CHAPTER ONE:

A Topsy-Turvy World 18

CHAPTER TWO:

All Is Bright: Decorating 52

CHAPTER THREE:

Gifts & Greetings 112

CHAPTER FOUR:

Christmas Is in Your Hands 188

AFTERWORD 225

ACKNOWLEDGMENTS 231

SOURCES 235

Introduction

Christmas has a way of making us wistful for the past. Even when
I was a kid, longing for an orange-and-black Garfield telephone
during the gadget-obsessed 1980s, Santa Claus himself was pretty
low tech. He may have brought us newfangled toys, but his accou
terments never seemed to change: the sleigh, the red suit, and the
handwritten thank-you notes left near the tableau of cookies and
carrots we'd put out for him and his eight reindeer on December 24.

My memories are steeped in old-fashioned details: decorating
our trees with vintage ornaments from different generations of
my family (mercury glass from my grandparents, hand-stitched
felt from my parents) and arranging our terra-cotta santons just
so. Modeled on Provençal villagers, these figurines celebrate the
baby Jesus in typically French fashion: by bringing wine, fresh

Opposite, main: Alaskan reindeer pull Santa's sled during the Pageant of Peace, Washington, DC, 1957. Photo by Volkmar
K. Wentzel/National Geographic/Getty Images. Opposite, far left top: Theodore Geisel, American writer and cartoonist,
at work on *How the Grinch Stole Christmas*, 1957. Photo by Al Ravenna, *World Telegram and Sun.* Library of Congress
Prints and Photographs Division, Washington, DC. Opposite, far left bottom: Christmas trees and wreaths in store window display, 1941–42. Library of Congress Prints and Photographs Division, Washington, DC.

baguettes, and other things to eat and drink. There were lots of contemporary touches, like plastic tinsel and certain beloved holiday specials like *A Charlie Brown Christmas*, but overall, the experience was almost like time travel back to a period in which people baked, sang, and generally made their own fun with a minimum of technology.

That's why I was intrigued a few years ago when I stumbled upon an article about Soviet-era New Year's cards that depicted Santa Claus's Cold War counterpart, Grandfather Frost, riding rocket ships and delivering presents from low orbit.

With a little digging, I started to discover that our own Santa Claus had dabbled in space travel, too. There are traces of it evident today: NORAD still "tracks" Santa on radar, as it has since 1955.

The period from 1945 to 1970 took Christmas in America (and, indeed, New Year's celebrations in the USSR) on a sharp detour away from the Victorian charm of the Christmases that so many of us remember, even those of us who grew up at the end of the Cold War or right after it. It's a funny exercise in futuristic nostalgia, like observing how the set and props of

Cover, *Weather Bureau Topics*, December 1958.
National Oceanic and Atmospheric Administration Central Library.

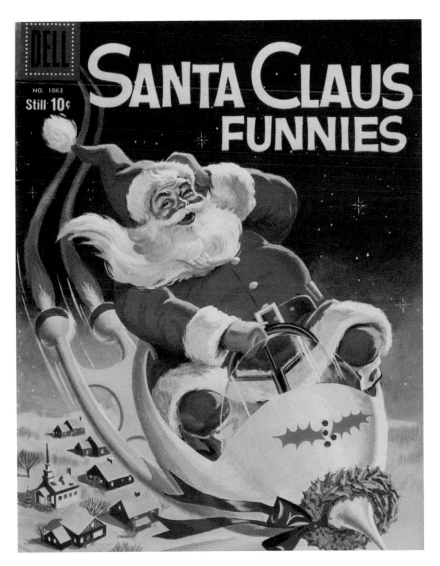

Cover of the Dell *Santa Claus Funnies*, December 1959, Western Printing & Litho Company.

Introduction

ntertaining Gifts

fun to give or receive—a delight for all ages

Color TV brings amazingly vivid, life-like programs. See big rectangular picture sizes, easier-than-ever color tuning.

Clock Radio lulls and wakes you to music, provides day-long pleasure as well.

Console Stereo adds dimension to records and radio, style to your home. Some have built-in tape recorder.

2

"Treasury of Christmas Ideas," Western Light and Telephone Company Home Services Department, 1960s. Lincoln Electric System.

the original *Star Trek* series anticipate our present-day technologies, even as it all looks very dated. Fueled by a sense of optimism and widespread prosperity, postwar Americans embraced a high-tech version of a holiday that had long been steeped in ancient lore and symbols of an old-fashioned way of life: sleighs, candles, handmade toys, and the worship of trees.

In the mid-1960s, a crackling Yule log glowed from Zenith television sets, and Christmas trees fashioned from shiny aluminum sparkled in the winter light. There are lots of reasons for this, but taken together, the enthusiasm for new materials, science, space travel, bold graphics, and a special love of convenience foods paint a picture of a society that was exhilarated by the possibilities of its new superpower status and a bit tentative, even frightened, of the postwar world it now occupied. The material culture and popular entertainment of the era put a brave face on it all, but the mysteries of space exploration, atomic energy, and the prospect of armed conflicts with the Soviet Union were very frightening to contemplate. This curious mixture of economic security and global anxiety made Americans want to nest like never before; the most extreme iteration of this impulse was the iconic home bomb shelter stocked with board games and canned goods.

In every era, the celebration of Christmas elicits a sense of wonder and childlike glee in adults and children alike. Each holiday season, the Christmas story reminds us that our own families and circles of friends are their own sorts of miracles to be celebrated. We cultivate a sense of magic around the holiday to remind ourselves of our good fortune, or to make manifest our hopes for better times to come. In the postwar era, a space-faring Santa, ultra-mod Christmas cards, wrapping paper, aluminum trees, and an array of scientific and domestically inspired toys gave tentatively optimistic Americans a way to make the Space Age their own, even familiar and cozy; something to behold in awe, not something to fear.

In 1957, Theodor Geisel, better known as Dr. Seuss, introduced American readers to their very own Atomic Age Scrooge: the Grinch, a sinister green critter who hated Christmas so much

he vowed to "steal" it from the cheery citizens of Whoville, as though Christmas itself were a commodity for sale at a department store.

Geisel's beloved holiday tale, which has since been adapted for television, film, and Broadway, was intended as a good-natured but serious critique of postwar America's love affair with all the commercial trappings of the holiday season. The inspiring moral of *How the Grinch Stole Christmas!* is that Christmas isn't a thing to be stolen at all, but a celebration of family and good cheer that arrives on cue every December, presents or no presents.

Charles Dickens's 1843 holiday masterpiece, *A Christmas Carol*, gave us the classic Christmas antihero, Ebenezer Scrooge: a cruel taskmaster, ungenerous toward his sympathetic employee, Bob Cratchit, and his family. When Scrooge sees the light on Christmas morning after he's visited by the ghosts of

Left: *Mister Magoo's Christmas Carol*, NBC Television, December 18, 1962. Directed by Abe Levitow.
Shown at left: Ebenezer Scrooge/Mr. Magoo (voice: Jim Backus). Photofest, Inc.

Right: *How the Grinch Stole Christmas!*, CBS Television, December 23, 1966. Directed by Chuck Jones and Ben Washam.
Shown: Max, the one-horned reindeer dog, and the Grinch (voice by Boris Karloff). Photofest, Inc.

Christmas Past, Present, and Future, he responds by sharing his material abundance with strangers and colleagues alike: gifts for the Cratchit children, a Christmas turkey, and a long-overdue raise for Bob. It's a happy ending that made perfect sense in Dickens's time, when things like unregulated child labor and urban poverty were pressing issues in Great Britain. Scrooge's Christmas enlightenment underscores the idea—relatively new at the time—that material prosperity should be shared by everyone.

The Grinch's tale wraps up very differently: In a climate of planned obsolescence, new shopping malls, mail-order catalogs, department store Santas, and television programming designed around commercials, Geisel's message to American readers was that none of us really needs presents—a new dishwasher, a new car, or any of the glittering decorations that signal the arrival of Christmas each December. Geisel's book was wildly popular, but his message was only partially received. During the postwar era, Americans shopped, decorated, and feasted like never before, making new, formerly exotic materials and technologies an integral part of this well-loved holiday. By the 1950s, more Americans than ever before could consider themselves middle class, and novel materials like plastic and aluminum made the look and feel of Christmas decidedly modern. By the 1960s, a typical Christmas tableau in a department store window might look more like the Jetsons than the Cratchits.

So how did this happen, and why was it temporary? Though it looked quite different, the atmosphere of newness, experimentation, and fun that charac-terized postwar Christmas celebrations echoed the spirit of the holiday's very earliest ancestors.

Left: Nela Park GE Lighting illuminated greeting cards, Cleveland, Ohio, 1958.

Right, top: Nela Park GE Lighting entrance decorated for Christmas, Cleveland, Ohio, 1936.

Right, bottom: Nela Park GE Lighting engineering building decorated for Christmas, Cleveland, Ohio, 1949.

Images reproduced with permission from GE Lighting, a business of General Electric Company.

Introduction

CHAPTER ONE

A Topsy-Turvy World

THE ROMAN SATURNALIA.—From drawing by J. R. Weguelin.

"The Roman Saturnalia," illustration by John Reinhard Weguelin, 1884.
Art and Picture Collection, The New York Public Library Digital Collections.

The Christmas season was historically a time of playful role reversal, and it has long had a kind of frenzied "final exams" quality to it—a natural phenomenon that dates back to the time when the cycles of farming governed the calendar. By early December, crops have been harvested, animals have been fattened up, and beer has been fermented. There's food and drink to be had, and not all that much work to do, so the natural impulse is to spend part of the month kicking back and enjoying the fruits of a season's hard labor.

During the ancient Roman festival of Saturnalia, celebrated every December, a public banquet was held in honor of the deity Saturn, who was associated with agriculture and wealth. Revelers feasted in the Roman Forum, and the party continued for days afterward. One of the key features of Saturnalia was role reversal: During the festival, slaves were treated like aristocrats, and aristocrats waited on their slaves. Gambling and playing dice, ordinarily against the law, were temporarily permitted. Gifts were exchanged, but they were usually of the sort we'd call "gag gifts"—good for

Christmas at the court of the Queen of England in 1848, after a contemporary lithograph. The Miriam and Ira D. Wallach Division of Art, Prints and Photographs: Print Collection, The New York Public Library Digital Collection.

a laugh, but relatively low cost. In other words, during this brief window of time in December, Roman society itself went topsy-turvy. And once everyone had cut loose and enjoyed themselves, it was time to reset the clock. This kind of role reversal only works if the social norms being temporarily turned upside down are understood as fixed and unchangeable. In the ancient world, as with medieval and early modern Europe, for the most part, they were.

In the fourth century A.D., when the early Church attempted to Christianize the revelry of Saturnalia season by setting the celebration of Christ's birth on December 25, the new holiday of Christmas inherited those customs. This was a deliberate attempt to curb the usual shenanigans of the season by devoting it to something pious and wholesome, but the results were mixed. The celebration of Christmas in Europe up until the age of the Puritans retained

many Saturnalia-like qualities, including the practice of wassailing, which was not the sort of cheery caroling we associate with Victorian times, but a bawdy (and sometimes even menacing) practice of what amounted to trick-or-treating by adults seeking food, beer, and cash. And, like the Romans, European peasants and landowners participated in their own version of a topsy-turvy season by staging Christmas revelries over which a character called the Lord of Misrule would preside. Christmas then was more like our contemporary Halloween: Men and women would swap clothing, children would dress up as famous adults and mock them, a peasant would take on the role of the Lord of Misrule and behave as though he were a landed gentlemen.

But a major element of this ritual is something we still strongly associate with Christmas today: charity. Christmas charity in medieval and Renaissance Europe wasn't the sort of no-strings-

"In the Parlor," Clement Clarke Moore, ca 1896. General Research Division,
The New York Public Library Digital Collections.

Previous, left: *Harper's Weekly* cover art by Edward Penfield, 1894. The Miriam and Ira D. Wallach Division of Art, Prints and Photographs: Print Collection, The New York Public Library Digital Collection.

Previous, center: *Harper's Christmas* cover art by Edward Penfield, 1894. The Miriam and Ira D. Wallach Division of Art, Prints and Photographs: Print Collection, The New York Public Library Digital Collection.

Previous, right: *Harper's Christmas* cover art by Edward Penfield, 1895. The Miriam and Ira D. Wallach Division of Art, Prints and Photographs: Print Collection, The New York Public Library Digital Collection.

attached donation of time and goods that we celebrate during the holidays now; it was more akin to defensive tipping. Lords would open their homes (the original Christmas open house) and invite the peasants in for a big meal, and in offering their bounty to the poor, they were reinforcing the existing social contract between those who owned the land and those who worked it. Suitably feted and acknowledged, the peasants offered in return their continued labor and loyalty. If all of this made a certain kind of sense in Europe, how did it translate into the New World? Well, it didn't, exactly.

It probably comes as no surprise that the Puritans hated Christmas. They didn't hate the idea of honoring the birth of Christ, of course, but they were horrified by the association between the religious observance of Christmas and the wild and woolly carnival atmosphere that took hold every December. The antics of the Lord of Misrule and the carousing of wassailers served to draw the focus away from religious observance, training people's attention on the pleasures of the flesh instead. The Massachusetts General Court declared the observance of Christmas a crime in 1659. There was no evidence in the Bible to support a December 25 Christmas celebration, least of all one that involved heavy drinking. It would take centuries for the holiday to transform from a winter feast for adults into a wholesome family holiday that centered around children.

The extreme makeover of Christmas began in early nineteenth-century New York City. In a sense, the upside-down world of Saturnalia was becoming the new reality year-round in America: Old aristocratic fortunes were fading, new industrial ones were emerging, and suddenly social class was fluid and dynamic, rather than fixed and permanent. Established power brokers and landowners were unnerved by the new lords of misrule in their midst: recent immigrants. The customs of old Christmas were in full force in the New World, but there was something different in the tone of the celebration that felt ominous. The stakes had changed: Instead of peasants, these new wassailers worked in factories and shipyards, and they could be laid off in midwinter if business slowed or the rivers froze. So the formalized exchange of goodwill that characterized the old interactions between landowners and peasants was suddenly fraught with the anxiety of a new economy in which the fear of insecure work fueled class resentment. A small group of influential New York businessmen took charge of Christmas in an effort to stem the tide of ill feeling and cultivate a sense of harmony in their diverse and rapidly expanding city.

Santa Claus climbed down an American chimney for the very first time in the year 1837. We know the exact date of this event because that's the year the scholar and philanthropist Clement Clarke Moore wrote the poem "A Visit from St. Nicholas," better known today by its first line, "'Twas the Night Before Christmas." Most of the familiar elements are there: stockings hanging over the fireplace, a deceptively agile St. Nicholas braving soot and the tight dimensions of a nineteenth-century chimney to descend into the living room, the muffled clattering of reindeer hooves on the roof, and sleepy children fantasizing about candy. The house is filled with a sense of quiet anticipation that not even a mouse frantically stirring fruitcake batter in the kitchen could disturb. Moore quite literally set the scene for a different kind of Christmas celebration, one in which, instead of adults from different social classes engaging in playful role reversal and letting off steam, a new population took center stage: children.

Moore wrote "A Visit from St. Nicholas" with a group of men, fellow elites who were known as the Knickerbockers. The writer Washington Irving had written his *A Knickerbocker's History of New York* in 1809, and in it St. Nicholas is depicted as a kindly, pipe-smoking figure. Moore and company adopted the figure of St. Nicholas in their mission to reshape the culture of Christmas, layering it with a "pseudo-Dutch" heritage for their city, one that emphasized a folksy, simpler time and place. Irving depicted St. Nicholas in *A Knickerbocker's History* as the patron saint of New Amsterdam. While St. Nicholas's original role as a bishop—a religious figure who can mete out justice to adults who have sinned—was part and parcel of his old identity, Moore's poem recasts St. Nicholas as a kindly, almost grandfatherly figure who judges children. Rather than a stern allegory of Judgment Day, the Christmas tradition of children being called to account for their behavior was understood as something being done in good fun, lumps of coal notwithstanding. In Moore's poem, St. Nick's eyes "twinkle," and he's rotund and jolly, rather than slim, judgmental, or serious. He also smokes what's described as a "stump of a pipe," which was a signal of low status in the eighteenth and nineteenth centuries. In other words, he's been transformed from a bishop with religious authority to a peasant full of no-strings-attached good cheer.

IF THEY KEEP MOVING THE CHRISTMAS SEASON UP EARLIER AND EARLIER, AN ADDED FUNCTION OF THE HOME AIR-CONDITIONER WILL BE KEEPING THE YULETIDE TREE FRESH AND GREEN THROUGHOUT AUGUST AND THE WARM EARLY SEPTEMBER WEEKS.

THIS IS THE TIME OF YEAR WHEN POST-OFFICES, DEPARTMENT STORES, AND CHILDREN'S EYES STAY OPEN LATER.

HOPE THIS BOOK OF CHRISTMAS QUIPS HAS BROUGHT A SMILE OR TWO AND THE HOLIDAYS WILL ALL ADD UP TO HAPPY DAYS FOR YOU!

MERRY CHRISTMAS

Hallmark Christmas Card, 1960s. Courtesy of Hallmark Cards, Inc.

A Topsy-Turvy World

ON THE LOOK OUT

FOR GOOD CHILDREN

SANTA CLAUS

HERE HE COMES!

HIS WORKS.

WORK-SHOP.

HOLIDAY WEEK

DOLLIES' TEA PARTY.

THE CHRISTMAS TREE.

DOLLIES' KITCHEN.

CHRISTMAS-EVE.

WHICH DOLLY WILL YOU HAVE?

DOLLIES' PARLOR.

Santa's Workshop

On December 25, 1866, Harper's Weekly published a cartoon by the popular illustrator Thomas Nast called "Santa Claus and His Works," which features a series of vignettes showing Santa in what we could consider his element. His "works" include decorating a Christmas tree, sewing doll clothes, making toys by hand in his carpenter's shop, scouting for good children (who are presumably hard to find) using a telescope, consulting an enormous "Record of Behavior" (described here using the argot of retail as an "account book"), and, of course, delivering presents near a moonlit fireplace.

His expanding girth is a reminder of the shift in the culinary focus of Christmas revelry away from alcoholic beverages for adults to sweets for children. He's shown in his workshop, depicted at a moment when the Industrial Revolution was humming at full speed, somehow making toys for every single one of the world's "good" children by using old-fashioned hand tools. And all of

"Santa Claus and His Works." Thomas Nast, *Harper's Weekly*, December 25, 1866.

this indoor revelry—sweets, gifts that appear as though by magic, and, by the mid-nineteenth century, Christmas trees—helped to shift the focus of Christmas celebration out of the streets and into the parlor. The old frenzy of revelry was now a new frenzy of consumption, and retailers took notice. Play was domesticated, and an effort to bring boys in particular indoors (or at least prevent them from hurling snowballs) led to a new marketplace for prepackaged games and game books, and special performances on Christmas Day designed just for children.

Gifts as far back as Roman Saturnalia had been mostly symbolic, and the gift exchange of the old-style Christmas was important more for its ritual symbolism than the monetary value of the item. All of this changed when Santa Claus began teaming up with department stores. Fueled by the buying power of an emerging middle class, both in Britain and the United States, the market for more costly and serious holiday gifts boomed. The rise of print advertising, increasing newspaper and magazine circulations, and the ability of department stores all over the country to stock goods from the coasts shipped via river or railroad meant that the whole population

American Christmas Card, ca. 1930s. Art and Picture Collection, The New York Public Library Digital Collection.

was now participating in a nationwide ritual of retail. Christmas had the ability to connect commerce with holiness and family in a way that no other holiday could match. Fancy clothes, jewelry, and books were the top choices for gifts given to adults, and sweets and toys were often given to children. The thrifty ethos of the early republic was being steadily chipped away by a new custom that made consumerism itself a form of patriotism; concern about economic hard times and the use of Santa as a personification of a holiday-driven economic recovery appeared in print as early as the 1830s.

Santa's retail power was subtle and almost counterintuitive: By disguising the machinery of consumer culture in an old-fashioned, preindustrial toy workshop, retailers could navigate around any latent tendencies toward Yankee thrift in the service of holiday cheer. In 1870, Christmas became a federal holiday in the United States, and Louis Prang produced the first Christmas cards in 1875. Santa's presence in department stores—a new market for wrapping paper, cards, and holiday decor for the home—flourished, and mail-order retailers like Sears® began producing colorful Christmas catalogs to tempt children and guide parents' holiday shopping.

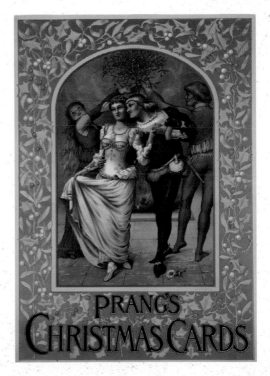

Print advertisement for Prang's Christmas Cards, ca. 1886. Library of Congress Prints and Photographs Division, Washington, DC.

American Christmas Card, 1900. Art and Picture Collection, The New York Public Library Digital Collection.

American Christmas Card, 1940. Art and Picture Collection, The New York Public Library Digital Collection.

Make Do and Mend

The traditional Christmas wish for peace on earth was especially poignant during World War II, when so many American families had loved ones overseas. The war effort on the home front included rationing, which meant that shoppers could purchase only small amounts of grocery staples like meat, dairy, coffee, sugar, and canned goods. Materials like rubber, metal, and gasoline were rationed too, with nylon stockings famously hard to come by. Americans were encouraged to "make do and mend": Conserve energy at home and in the car, tailor clothing to use as little fabric as possible, and recycle or reuse household goods and materials. Coming as it did on the heels of the Great Depression, this kind of household thrift was already familiar to most Americans, and indeed, many felt proud to be doing their part in helping the war effort.

Rationing meant scaling way back on all the things that had been associated with Christmas since the mid-nineteenth century: food and drink, material goods, the energy needed to power decorative

Christmas in Connecticut, 1945. Directed by Peter Godfrey. Shown from left: Barbara Stanwyck, Dennis Morgan. Photofest, Inc.

lights, and even the use of the telephone for making long-distance calls. Since gasoline was rationed, travel was restricted, and annual visits to family in neighboring states had to be postponed.

The bittersweet experience of wartime Christmas in America was captured by hit songs like "White Christmas" by Irving Berlin, first aired in 1941; Bing Crosby's "I'll Be Home For Christmas," written for troops in 1943; and "Have Yourself a Merry Little Christmas," from the 1944 movie musical *Meet Me in St. Louis*. In the movie, Judy Garland is costumed to look like a Gilded Age teenager in turn-of-the-century Missouri, but when she sang, "From now on, our troubles will be miles away," wartime listeners and moviegoers understood what she meant.

Americans were encouraged—by the Office of War Information and, curiously, by corporations—to do without things and to spend their money on war bonds instead of gifts. Some companies capitalized on this by offering products in tandem with the purchase of war bonds. In the issue of *LIFE* magazine from June 11, 1944, an ad for The Hoover Company explained that the company was making war equipment instead of vacuum cleaners, and used its

Hedrich Blessing Photographers, window display at Marshall Field & Company, 1943. HB-07632-H. Chicago History Museum, Chicago, Illinois.

Santa Claus has gone to War !

YOUR GIFT – PLENTY OF WEAPONS
The INLAND Way for U.S.A.

Office for Emergency Management War Production Board, ca. 1942-43. "Santa Claus Has Gone To War." National Archives and Records Administration, Special Media Archives Services Division (NWCS-S).

Left: Hedrich Blessing Photographers, window display at Marshall Field & Company, 1943. HB-07654-A. Chicago History Museum, Chicago, Illinois.

Right: Hedrich Blessing Photographers, window display at Marshall Field & Company, 1943. HB-07717-C. Chicago History Museum, Chicago, Illinois.

paid ad space to share tips on how readers could make their homes "war-shortening households" by conserving and reusing materials. Magazines like *Woman's Day*, *Better Homes and Gardens*, and *House Beautiful* began publishing ideas for how to make holiday decorations and ornaments by hand, using non-rationed materials. Powdered Lux soap could be used to make convincing fake snow, and even natural objects like shells or pinecones could be fashioned into ornaments. After the war, companies that made materials that had previously been rationed, like Reynolds Metals (aluminum foil) or DuPont (cellophane) began advertising ways to use these new materials in DIY holiday decorating projects, and magazines followed suit, carrying on an inventive wartime tradition in the era of postwar abundance.

The war caused shifts in production from Europe to America in all sorts of industries. New York Fashion Week was established as a homegrown alternative to the Paris shows during the war, altering the course of the American fashion industry long after the conflict ended. The same held true for Christmas decorations. In the nineteenth and early twentieth centuries, Germany was the world capital of Christmas manufacturing across all categories: tinsel, ornaments, toys, games, and the revival of the Christmas tree itself in the 1830s. During World War II and after, American companies began producing toys and decorations on their own, even finding ingenious ways to adapt existing equipment. After the war began, the Corning Glass Works began making Christmas ornaments using a machine that had originally been designed to produce lightbulbs. At peak efficiency, the Corning method could produce more ornaments in a minute than a German glassblower could produce by hand in a day.

Buy Gifts in Cellophane

DELUXE SMOKING BLEND

Holiday fruit cake

et Cellophane add glamour to your Christm

Wrap Gifts in Cellophane

And Cellophane for decorations too!

Cellophane Garlands and Roping to decorate your house or tree.

Cellophane Wreaths—plain and electrical — colorful and sparkling — reflect Christmas

Decorate with Nature's gifts *continued*

Use Traditional Christmas materials, but give them a Contemporary flair

You'll enjoy this white "poinsettia" all winter. Paint magnolia or any large flat leaves and spray with canned snow while paint is wet. When dry, thread leaves at base on fine wire and coil around pinon cone. Touch top of cone with glue and glitter

Natural greens, cones, and gilded gourd "bells" make up this spirited centerpiece. Directions for bells are on page 155. For a really festive touch use red felt tablecloth and Noel candle blocks. China is Ranier Pine pattern with Alpine tumblers

Much of the beauty of this handsome Della Robbia wreath—designed for a persimmon red door— lies in the stunning color combinations. Fruit, berries, and foliages are securely fastened to a firm background frame. Directions are on page

Photographs: Weymouth; Hopkins; de Gennaro

Set the stage for the meeting of good friends. At your holiday open-house gatherings, use a lovely ensemble of natural greens. The wall wreath, miniature pine-tree pillars in raffia wrapped and a flat, narrow table swag give Christmas glamor to cranberry punch served from a milk-glass bowl in matching

An espaliered Christmas tree studded with oranges and glitter creates a striking effect in the Contemporary room. Apples, or any smooth, clean-lined fruit may be substituted to fit an

Opposite: Advertisement for DuPont cellophane, 1949. Hagley Museum and Library, Wilmington, Delaware.

Left: Originally published in *Better Homes and Gardens®* magazine, December 1956.

Merry and Modern

The period that immediately followed the end of the Second World War transformed the United States socially, economically, politically, and visually. Not only did it feel different, everything looked different too. Part of this was the change in the physical landscape, which blossomed with new subdivisions and tract houses during the suburban building boom, but it was also thanks to the new look of postwar modernism coupled with the aesthetics of the Space Age.

After the war, with industrial productivity at an all-time high, American consumers could afford gifts and decorations on a much larger scale; the customs of the well-to-do could now belong to almost everyone. The economist John Kenneth Galbraith wrote in 1958 that "the ordinary individual has access to amenities—foods, entertainment, personal transportation, and plumbing—in which not even the rich rejoiced a century ago."

Esther Williams wishing her fans a Merry Christmas, 1952. The Everett Collection.

Since the mid-nineteenth century, the celebration of Christmas in America had been an exercise in nostalgia, during which people living in a time of rapid industrialization and social change cultivated rituals that evoked an imagined, preindustrial past. But the Christmas season has also historically been a time for trying things on and switching things up, and reveling in the novelty of a topsy-turvy world. Once World War II was over, Americans developed a holiday culture that turned the old Victorian status quo upside down and made a Christmas wish for something new: the future.

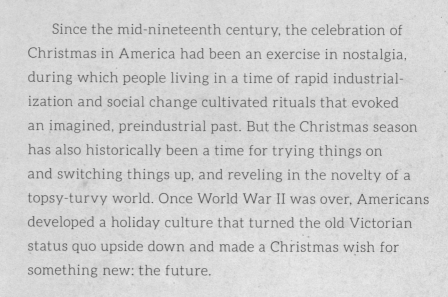

Atomic missile pedal car, Murray Ohio Manufacturing Company, 1958. Courtesy of The Strong, Rochester, New York.

Midcentury Christmas

"It's Christmas Again," print advertisement for The Airlines of the United States, 1945. Reproduced with permission from Airlines for America.

It's Christmas Again

ITS been a long time since the last real Christmas. *This one* we can celebrate with something near the old-time joy. True, the world bears scars that will never heal. To millions, something has gone out of life forever. But no amount of human suffering can dim the star that shed its gracious lustre on the Prince of Peace.

Bringing the world ever closer together in its quest for peace is the airplane. It flies just as quickly from hemisphere to hemisphere on missions of good will as on missions of war. Never has the nation or the world stood to gain more from science and invention than it does today from air transportation.

Airport terminals all over this nation and over the world are again thronged with people, light hearted and gay, hastening home in swift flight to gleaming hearthfires and the laughter of children and the tinkle of bells on the evergreen boughs.

A MERRY CHRISTMAS EVERYONE
... and a thousand glad New Years to come!

Air Transport Association, 1515 Massachusetts Avenue, N. W., Washington 5, D. C.

This advertisement is sponsored by the nation's airlines and leading manufacturers in the aviation industry

THE AIRLINES OF THE UNITED STATES
LEADING THE WORLD IN AIR TRANSPORT

Left: An illuminated Santa figurine, Paramount, 1950s–1960s. Photo by Jeffrey Stockbridge.

Right: An American Christmas card, 1950s.

Opposite: *White Christmas* poster, 1954. Shown: Rosemary Clooney, Bing Crosby, Danny Kaye, and Vera-Ellen. The Everett Collection.

A STORY WITH LAUGHTER AND HEART... TO THRILL ALL AGES... AGAIN... AND AGAIN!

THE MUSIC, THE MAGIC OF ONE OF THE GREATEST ENTERTAINERS OF ALL TIME!

IRVING BERLIN'S WONDERFUL "WHITE CHRISTMAS"

BING CROSBY • DANNY KAYE
ROSEMARY CLOONEY • VERA-ELLEN

DEAN JAGGER · Lyrics and Music by IRVING BERLIN · Produced by ROBERT EMMETT DOLAN · Directed by MICHAEL CURTIZ · Dances and Musical Numbers Staged by Robert Alton · Written for the screen by NORMAN KRASNA, NORMAN PANAMA and MELVIN FRANK · A PARAMOUNT PICTURE · VISTAVISION · TECHNICOLOR

White Christmas, 1954. Directed by Michael Curtiz, starring Rosemary Clooney, Danny Kaye, Bing Crosby, and Vera-Ellen. Photofest, Inc.

Opposite: Jane Russell trimming a Christmas tree, 1951. Photofest, Inc.

A Topsy-Turvy World

CHAPTER TWO

All Is Bright: Decorating

For kids, or adults who have a pretty low-key shopping list, the days and weeks that lead up to Christmas are almost as much fun as the day itself—even more fun, in a sense, because they're bursting with anticipation. The rituals of decorating and baking help distract us. Many of my favorite Christmas memories are actually of the lead up, rather than the day itself: bringing out boxes of ornaments, unwrapping the Nativity set, opening new packages of tinsel (only to find pieces of it months later hiding in crevices all over the living room). Learning the tricks of the trade as a child, like how to string Christmas tree lights the right way or bake gingerbread, makes one feel skilled in a culturally specific way, like part of the tribe. And no matter the style of one's holiday tableau, we have the postwar era to thank for many of these rituals and the material conveniences that make the monthlong marathon of decor and entertaining more streamlined; after all, spending cozy time at home was at the center of midcentury life.

Opposite: In the upscale department store I. Magnin, guards keep a careful watch over a bejeweled Christmas tree as a well-dressed customer admires the $1.5 million worth of gems that decorate it.
Los Angeles, California, December 1955. Photo by Allan Grant/The LIFE Picture Collection/Getty Images.

Right: Assorted ornament hangers from the 1950s and 1960s. Photo by Jeffrey Stockbridge.

All Is Bright: Decorating

Jiminy Christmas! What a g...

THE GENERAL ELECTRIC SPACE MAKER REFRIGERATOR

MERRY CHRISTMAS to the family

Why Nest?

The American Dream had a golden age: 1945–73, to be exact. What began with a burst of unprecedented economic prosperity following the end of World War II ended with the 1973 oil embargo, which unfolded against the backdrop of the Watergate hearings and a dreamy soundtrack of Elton John and The Carpenters classics.

The postwar boom years totally transformed the way Americans thought about house and home. In 1940, 43.6 percent of Americans owned their home. By 1960, 61.9 percent did. This was due in large measure to the benefits of the Servicemen's Readjustment Act of 1944, better known as the G.I. Bill, which gave returning soldiers funding to start new businesses, attend college or graduate school, and obtain home mortgages. In 1947, developer William Levitt built the first of many "Levittowns" on 4,000 acres of Long Island farmland. Across the country, home building in new suburbs proliferated. In 1944, 114,000 new homes were built, and in 1950, that figure was 1.7 million.

The focus on home and hearth was not new during the postwar era; the nineteenth century gave rise to what historians call the

Advertisement for the General Electric Space Maker Refrigerator, December 1948.
Reproduced with permission from GE Lighting, a business of General Electric Company.

"cult of domesticity," as industrialization increasingly split men's and women's roles between the outside world of business and commerce and the interior world of family, housework, and nurturance. But Americans did have a good new reason to fixate on the domestic front. With Great Britain ravaged by the war even in victory, the two new superpowers that emerged in 1945—the United States and the Soviet Union—were both large, formidable, and ideologically opposed to one another on the basis of their respective economic systems. Newfound prosperity coupled with worry about possible conflict with the Soviets meant that middle-class homeowners doubled down on domesticity. Their increased buying power drove sales of home appliances and improvements to rates far higher than the consumption of other goods like clothing, travel, or entertainment. In 1958, Bank of America unveiled the first consumer credit card, and by 1960 there were more than 100 million of them in use in the United States.

Pundits characterized Communism as a threat not just to the American way of life in general, but to the American family unit in particular; the ideology of shared resources undercut the nesting instinct of American parents to provide for their kids and build a secure, happy home. The hyperfocus on what we now think of as an idealized family unit as seen on *Leave it to Beaver* makes sense in this light: Faced with the prospect of a frightening global conflict waged across the Iron Curtain, coziness wasn't just comforting, it was patriotic. So for Americans who had put their spending habits on hold since the stock market crash of 1929, the end of World War II meant happy days were here again, at long last. Threat of nuclear conflict and proliferation of things like the home bomb shelter led to two places peo-

House Beautiful, December 1963. Reprinted with permission of Hearst Communications, Inc.

ple in the American suburbs could focus their attention: the home and its myriad stylish conveniences, and the faraway world of technology, atomic energy, and the space race. In 1948, before his name became synonymous with suburban tract houses, William Levitt summarized it perfectly: "No man who owns his own house and lot can be a Communist. He has too much to do."

С НОВЫМ ГОДОМ!

С Новым годом!

New Year's cards from the USSR, 1960s and 1970s.

Opposite: *House Beautiful*, December 1961. Reprinted with permission of Hearst Communications, Inc.

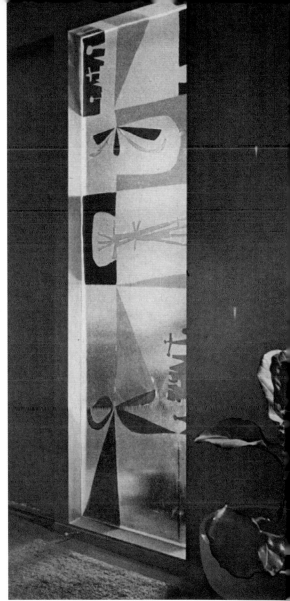

House Beautiful, December 1954. Reprinted with permission of Hearst Communications, Inc.

All Is Bright: Decorating

House Beautiful, December 1963. Reprinted with permission of Hearst Communications, Inc.

House Beautiful, December 1954. Reprinted with permission of Hearst Communications, Inc.

Our Friend the Atom

The 1950s introduced new technology to the world, and with it a whole new visual vocabulary, much of it derived from efforts by designers and illustrators to make complex scientific ideas clear to a wide range of people. Postwar America was living through the age of the atom; though scientific understanding of the structure and behavior of atoms dates all the way back to the turn of the twentieth century, the 1950s and '60s became known as the Atomic Age because the end of World War II made nuclear energy part of a national conversation. Cold War anxiety about the possibility of armed conflict with the Soviets coupled with the thrilling possibilities of a nuclear-powered society meant this technology was something people had to get used to, one way or another. Like electricity before it, the awesome power of nuclear energy was communicated to a wide audience through the design of objects, graphics, and animation. A 1956 book by German physicist Dr. Heinz Haber,

Walt Disney consults with Dr. Heinz Haber during the making of *Our Friend the Atom*. California, ca. 1957. Photo by Gene Lester/Getty Images.

Our Friend the Atom, and its companion episode of the TV series *Disneyland*, painted a serious but optimistic picture of atomic energy for young viewers by interpreting its power through a modern retelling of "The Fisherman and the Genie," one of the stories told by Scheherazade in *One Thousand and One Nights*. Atomic power is the proverbial "genie in the bottle," and the "three wishes" are the (rather idealized) benefits that nuclear energy can offer mankind: power, food and health, and peace.

The stylized model of the atom comprised of three or four ovals through which one or more dots appear to "orbit" became visual shorthand for both nuclear power itself and a more general kind of scientific progress that seemed zippy and exciting. It was used as the logo of the United States Atomic Energy Commission, which existed from 1946 to 1974, and is more recognizable today as the logo of the Apple Genius Bar. Atoms were in the zeitgeist in the 1950s and '60s, appearing in toys and comic books, in the design of lighting fixtures and tableware. This design perfectly complemented the forms and aesthetics of modernism, the early twentieth-century movement that eschewed ornament and embraced abstraction, basic forms, and bold color.

To imagine the architectural style sometimes referred to as the Googie movement, named for a now-defunct California coffee shop designed by architect John Lautner in 1949, picture neon-lit road signs with zigzag or starburst details, or a hamburger stand with a big sweeping roof shaped like a parabola. Googie landmarks include Betty Willis's iconic 1959 "Welcome to Fabulous Las Vegas" sign, Edward E. Carlson and John Graham Jr.'s Space Needle in Seattle, and Eero Saarinen's TWA Flight Center in New York City. The Space Needle and the TWA Flight Center were both built in 1962. *The Jetsons'* cartoon space-home

also could be characterized as Googie design. The stylized
Atomic Age imagery that evoked speed, movement, and
light was also inherently festive, and it was quickly adopted
by the designers of Christmas cards, wrapping paper, and
toys, giving midcentury Christmas celebrations a brand-
new look. Even the old-fashioned Christmas tree and its
sparkling glass ornaments were suddenly cutting edge. The
humble Christmas ball might just be the perfect postwar
holiday object: round, conical, or teardrop-shaped, brightly
colored, abstract, and light as a feather, these Christmas
ornaments somehow anticipated the aesthetics of the
Atomic Age by at least a century.

Three glass Christmas ornaments
manufactured by Corning Glass
Works, ca. 1940s–60s. Collec-
tion of The Corning Museum of
Glass, Corning, New York. Gift of
Pat Brarens.

House Beautiful, December 1961. Reprinted with permission of Hearst Communications, Inc.

Assorted Shiny Brite ornaments from the 1950s and 1960s, shown on a vintage aluminum Christmas tree.
Photo by Jeffrey Stockbridge.

All Is Bright: Decorating

Ornaments

The origin of the Christmas ball can be traced to Germany, which in the nineteenth and early twentieth century was the global capital of Christmas production. Evergreen Christmas trees had long been decorated in Germany and elsewhere in Northern Europe with edible treats like pastries, candy, and apples—all symbols of festive abundance to be enjoyed during the coldest months. Though it can't be proven beyond doubt, it seems likely that the idea of a shiny glass "apple" to decorate Christmas trees symbolized the spirit of the season: a piece of fruit that would never go bad glimmering from a tree that would never turn brown.

Christmas balls—or "baubles," as they're also called—were first made from glass in the town of Lauscha, Germany, where Christoph Müller and Hans Greiner established the region's first glass workshop in 1597. Here, the craftsmen made drinking glasses, bowls, flasks, and beads. A later artisan named Hans Greiner, a direct descendent of one of the workshop's original

Opposite, top: Ornaments being decorated at the Corning Glassworks, Courtesy of the Corning Incorporated Department of Archives & Records Management, Corning, New York.

Opposite, bottom: Striped-top Christmas ornament manufactured by Corning Glass Works, ca. 1940s–60s. Collection of The Corning Museum of Glass, Corning, New York. Gift of Roland Henry Peterson and Mary Nelson Peterson.

Boxed set of Christmas ornaments manufactured by Corning Glass Works, 1950s. Collection of the Corning Museum of Glass, Corning, New York. Gift of Jane E. Preston.

Outdoor decorating kit manufactured by Corning Glass Works, 1967-73. Collection of the Corning Museum of Glass, Corning, New York. Gift of Joy R. Hoffman.

Midcentury Christmas

founders, began making glass Christmas baubles there in 1847, around the time that Christmas trees were enjoying an urban revival in Germany. Greiner's first glass ornaments were fruit-shaped, and he used a combination of glassblowing and molds to create them by hand. The earliest glass ornaments were made to appear silvery through the application of mercury or lead, but a combination of silver nitrate with sugar water was found to work better. Glass ornaments grew in popularity across Europe, and when an 1848 engraving depicting Queen Victoria's family gathered around a colorful Christmas tree decorated with the glass baubles circulated in popular print outlets, demand grew even more.

American retail tycoon F. W. Woolworth visited Germany in 1890s, and though he was initially reluctant to sell glass ornaments back home, his merchandising experiment paid off: By the middle of the 1890s, Woolworth's stores were selling about $25 million in baubles each year. World War I temporarily halted the import of German ornaments and other decorations to the United States, but production and sales resumed throughout the 1920s and '30s. An enterprising importer, however, sensed that with another war appearing increasingly likely, a bigger and more permanent change was afoot in the global economy. Max Eckardt, a native of Germany, had been successfully importing hand-painted glass Christmas ornaments from Bavaria since the 1920s, working out of a warehouse on the Harlem River in New York City. Selling them under the names Shiny Brite and Max Eckardt & Sons, Eckardt had relatives and employees in Germany silvering and decorating the ornaments by hand, applying glitter and color to figures of Santa Claus and his elves, lanterns, stars, and cozy cottages.

The mechanics of mass production favored a simpler shape, however, bringing the spherical Christmas bauble back into vogue. In 1937, Eckardt and a representative from F. W. Woolworth contacted the New York-based Corning Glass Works to see if they could produce ornaments in the United States. Corning was already becoming a household brand thanks to the success of Pyrex, and its executives were intrigued by the prospect of diversifying into the German-dominated Christmas market with war in Europe looming. Woolworth offered to place large orders for ornaments if they could figure out how to adapt their "ribbon machine," which Corning had been using to mass-produce lightbulbs since 1926, to make the new glass baubles. Woolworth ordered more than 235,000 ornaments, and in December 1939 the first American-made glass

ornaments were produced by Corning and sold in Woolworth's stores for a few cents each. In 1940, more than 45 million were sold. Corning also made "fancies," ornaments in the shapes of Santa Claus, elves, fruits, candy, and the like.

The ornament business was very good to Corning. A skilled German glassblower could produce about 600 ornaments per day; Corning was making several hundred thousand per day at its production plant in Wellsboro,

Print advertisement for Corning Christmas ornaments, 1940s. Courtesy of the Corning Incorporated Department of Archives & Records Management, Corning, New York.

Two-part Christmas ornament molds, manufactured by Corning Glass Works, Wellsboro, Pennsylvania, 1940–55.
Collection of the Corning Museum of Glass, Corning, New York. Gift of Susan W. Schwartz, PhD.

All Is Bright: Decorating

Assorted Shiny Brite ornaments from the 1950s and 1960s, shown in a vintage Shiny Brite box from the same period. Photo by Jeffrey Stockbridge.

Cardboard Christmas ornaments designed by Oliver Lincoln Lundquist and Julian von der Lancken for Norse Craft, Inc., 1956. Cooper Hewitt, Smithsonian Design Museum/Art Resource, New York.

Pennsylvania. Clear glass balls were shipped from Wellsboro to Max Eckardt's new decorating facility in New Jersey, where they would be hand-painted in luminous bright colors and boxed with the trade name Shiny Brite. The shapes of Shiny Brite ornaments, which began as perfect spheres, would eventually come to include more complex forms, painted with stripes and later what we would call "ombré" hues. They were silvered inside and out, with the promise that they would keep their "shiny, bright" glimmer for years to come, and remarkably, most of them have.

As with so many materials during World War II, silver was rationed, so clear glass balls were adorned with pastel-colored stripes that didn't use as much metallic pigment. Some World War II–era Shiny Brite balls were sold with cardboard caps for hanging, and customers frequently resorted to yarn to hang them from their trees. Shiny Brite ornaments reached peak popularity in the late 1950s, but faded somewhat with the advent of plastic ornaments from other manufacturers. Still, their sheer volume, thanks to decades of mass production, means they adorned millions of trees and can still be found in excellent condition on the vintage market.

Assorted ornament hangers from the 1950s and 1960s.
Photo by Jeffrey Stockbridge.

Graphic designer Robert Brownjohn (1925–1970) pushed the Christmas ball to its artistic limit when he created a waveform holiday sculpture for the lobby of Pepsi-Cola headquarters in New York City in 1958. The installation was composed of hundreds of Christmas balls in bright colors, arranged on a supporting structure that twisted and curled like a Möbius strip. Brownjohn was a founding member of the design firm now known as Chermayeff & Geismar & Haviv, and he was responsible for the iconic cover of the Rolling Stones' *Let it Bleed*, as well as the opening title sequences of the James Bond movies *Goldfinger* and *From Russia With Love*.

Robert Brownjohn, *Pepsi-Cola Convention Christmas Lobby Sculpture*, 1958–59. Gift of Don Goeman. © The Estate of Robert Brownjohn.
Image © The Museum of Modern Art/Licensed by SCALA/Art Resource, New York.

All Is Bright: Decorating

CHRISTMAS LIGHTING and DECORATING

GENERAL ⊕ ELECTRIC

Colorful "Multiple" Lamps

When one of these long-burning General Electric Christmas Tree lamps does burn out, the rest stay lit! No hunting around for burned-out lamps. In red, blue, orange, green and white, they'll make every tree sing with the spirit of Yuletide. Candelabra base. For multiple strings.

C-7½ Bulbs
Suggested retail price
10¢ each plus tax

G-14 Bulbs
Suggested retail price
20¢ each plus tax

4 Merry

More G-E Christ... this year than... demand, you m... want. Be sure t...

New ...
like bea... ornaments... tree is ligh... into gorgeo... ling beauty ir... Candelabra b... multiple Chris...

Famous Series "Pine Cone" Lamps

The majority of Christmas tree outfits use these slightly smaller, "pine-cone" shaped G-E lamps. For years their twinkling beauty has gemmed millions of Christmas trees and lighted decorations. Miniature base; made for "series" wiring only.

C-6 Bulbs
Suggested retail price
7¢ each plus tax

C-9½ Bulbs
Suggested retail price
13¢ each plus tax

G-E Chr...
Lamps for...
the produ...
constant c...

G·E LAMPS
GENERAL ⊕ ELECTRIC

Stay B...

T Ⓖ WAYS TO SAY

Christmas

...e lamps will be available
...fore. Yet so great is the
... be able to buy all you
... suggested retail prices.

...se G-E lamps look
...round colorful
...your Christmas
...en they spring
...iance! Spark-
...ndard colors.
...t any indoor
...ree string.

Outdoors! As beautiful as
a technicolor production of "Merry
Christmas" are these General
Electric Christmas Tree Lamps for
outdoor decoration. Colored on the
inside; prevents weather-fading,
chipping, scraping. Intermediate
base. For multiple outdoor strings.

... tree lamps, like all G-E
..., office and factory are
...-E Lamp Research whose
...o make all G-E Lamps . . .

...ghter Longer!

Lighting

If silvery glass ornaments made Christmas trees sparkle and shine, it was in the electric string light that the modern holiday display truly met its match. The rather dangerous practice of using real wax candles to illuminate Christmas trees originated around the same time as the tradition of decorating trees with edible treats. The packaging and advertisements for electric Christmas lights, which began to appear in limited quantities at the turn of the twentieth century, often touted their safety, as Christmas house fires were an all-too-common occurrence where real candles were used. Christmas lights, like electricity itself, took a few decades to become widespread, but by the 1920s, 85 percent of American homes were wired. According to Jeff Carter, a major collector of vintage Christmas lights, General Electric was an early leader in the field with its Mazda Lamps, along with NOMA, a company that was formed through the consolidation of fifteen smaller manufac-turers across the country.

Opposite, main: Advertisement for GE lamps, General Electric Company, 1947.

Opposite, top and bottom: "GE Christmas Lighting and Decorating Guide," 1963.
Images reproduced with permission from GE Lighting, a business of General Electric Company.

Though they were considered a luxury, during the Depression sales of electric Christmas lights grew somewhat, perhaps due to string lights' ability to lend a touch of cheery glamour to an outdoor party in nice weather or to a festive holiday tableau. In 1927, GE introduced the C9 outdoor Christmas bulb. By 1933, the coloring process was improved to make the colors more durable in winter weather. Like silvered Christmas baubles, they were painted from the inside. In the mid-1930s, GE unveiled the C7 lamp, which solved one of the major problems that afflicted early string lights: If one bulb burned out, the rest did too. This selling point would be adopted by other makers through the 1960s. Like most other manufacturers, both GE and NOMA temporarily devoted much of their production capacity to the war effort in the first half of the 1940s. In 1946, NOMA introduced its newest innovation, which had been on hold since the early 1940s: the Bubble Lite. Like an early lava lamp, the Bubble Lite flickered through a tube of liquid. More than 150 million Bubble Lites had sold by 1950.

The 1950s and '60s were the golden age of corporate advice, a practice related to but distinct from advertising. How-to

FRAYED

CHIPPED OR LOOSE

"GE Christmas Lighting and Decorating Guide," 1963. Reproduced with permission from GE Lighting, a business of General Electric Company.

Hy-Glow outdoor Christmas lights, 1960s.
Photo by Jeffrey Stockbridge.

NOMA Christmas lights, late 1930s–early 1940s.
Photo by Jeffrey Stockbridge.

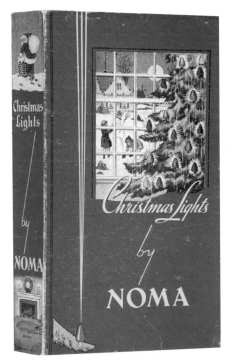

NOMA Christmas lights, late 1930s–early 1940s.
Photo by Jeffrey Stockbridge.

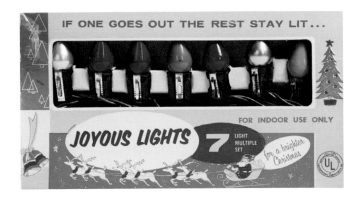

Joyous Christmas lights, 1950s.
Photo by Jeffrey Stockbridge.

All Is Bright: Decorating

"GE Christmas Lighting and Decorating Guide," 1963.
Reproduced with permission from GE Lighting, a business of General Electric Company.

Midcentury Christmas

Sales flier for GE Lighting, General Electric Company, 1963.
Reproduced with permission from GE Lighting, a business of General Electric Company.

manuals, idea "treasuries," and recipe booklets proliferated, offering consumers glossy magazine–style inspiration for how to decorate and make merry in their own homes. Resources like the *Popular Mechanics Christmas Handbook* from 1951 and Theodore Saros's *Christmas Lighting and Decorating* from 1954 both capitalized on this interest and gave serious lighting enthusiasts ideas to last a dozen holiday seasons. GE sponsored home-lighting contests and even provided guides for people who wanted to run their own competitions. All of this seemed to work, according to Carter: "In 1953 there were about 44 million households in the United States. In that year there were over 300 million Christmas lights sold—25 percent of them were used outdoors. Based on retail sales, decorative Christmas lighting was a $90 million industry."

GE also had the ultimate showplace for demonstrating products and stylish lighting ideas: Nela Park in Cleveland,

Ohio. Nela Park, the headquarters of GE Lighting, was first developed in 1911 by the National Electric Lamp Company (NELA) and later absorbed by GE.

The 92-acre complex was the first modern industrial park in the world and was designed in neo-Georgian style to resemble a college campus. In 1933, it became the home of GE's Lighting & Electrical Institute, and it quickly became a kind of outdoor holiday lighting laboratory for the company, whose holiday displays remain a tourist attraction to this day. Each year, a miniature version of the National Christmas Tree in Washington, D.C., designed by GE Lighting, is displayed at Nela Park.

Popular Mechanics Christmas Handbook, 1952. Reprinted with permission of Hearst Communications, Inc.

Holiday Displays at Nela Park, GE Lighting, 1950s.
Reproduced with permission from GE Lighting, a business of General Electric Company.

All Is Bright: Decorating

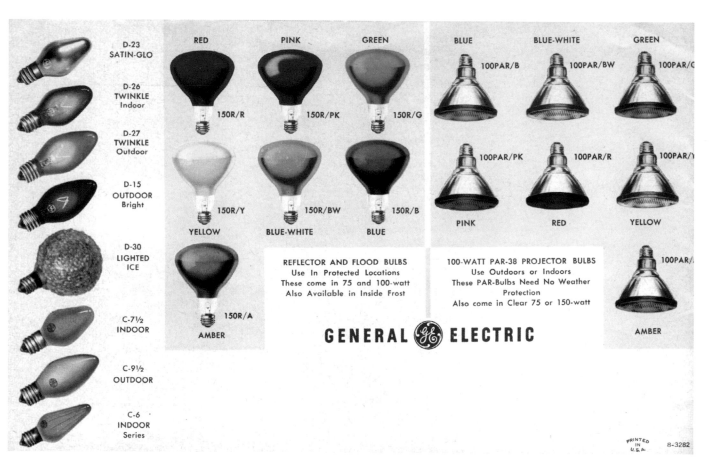

D-23 SATIN-GLO

D-26 TWINKLE Indoor

D-27 TWINKLE Outdoor

D-15 OUTDOOR Bright

D-30 LIGHTED ICE

C-7½ INDOOR

C-9½ OUTDOOR

C-6 INDOOR Series

RED — 150R/R

PINK — 150R/PK

GREEN — 150R/G

YELLOW — 150R/Y

BLUE-WHITE — 150R/BW

BLUE — 150R/B

AMBER — 150R/A

REFLECTOR AND FLOOD BULBS
Use In Protected Locations
These come in 75 and 100-watt
Also Available in Inside Frost

BLUE — 100PAR/B

BLUE-WHITE — 100PAR/BW

GREEN — 100PAR/G

100PAR/PK

100PAR/R

100PAR/Y

PINK

RED

YELLOW

100PAR/A

AMBER

100-WATT PAR-38 PROJECTOR BULBS
Use Outdoors or Indoors
These PAR-Bulbs Need No Weather
Protection
Also come in Clear 75 or 150-watt

GENERAL Ⓖ **ELECTRIC**

PRINTED IN U.S.A.

8-3282

"GE Christmas Lighting and Decorating Guide," 1963.
Reproduced with permission from GE Lighting, a business of General Electric Company.

Outdoors

There shouldn't be too many or too few lights on your Christmas tree whether it be inside or outside. Listed below are the rules for the minimum and maximum number of lights to use.

RULE FOR NUMBER
OF LAMPS TO USE.
3 × H × W = MAXIMUM
½ MAXIMUM = MINIMUM

Here is a different decorating technique using the new OUTDOOR BRIGHT (D15) lights especially designed for exterior use and viewing. Putting transparent lamps on a deciduous tree will make a pleasant contrast from neighbors decorations. The wreath is lighted by blue D15's in pie plate reflectors to give added brilliance. Colored spotlights are also used to give added light to the overall scene and to emphasize highlights.

7

Golden Snowflakes and a Galaxy of Stars that Twinkle

The two 'flakes (A) are made of cardboard and hardboard, ½" x 1" wood strips, C-7½ string sets and aluminum foil. Use compass and ruler to make snowflake patterns on paper. To transfer a design to cardboard, place a carbon sheet beneath the pattern and trace.

SOFT PINE   HARDBOARD
CARDBOARD

Snowflakes measure 18" x 24" and 14" x 18". When they have been wired and completed (B), hang on door by means of bailing wire and screw-eyes, as shown on page six.

Star reflectors can be cut from cardboard and covered with foil (C)—or plastic ones may be bought (D). Insulated staples hold two twinkle string sets (E) to porch walls at each socket; place reflectors over sockets and screw in lamps. Use PAR-38 floods for over-all attractiveness.

"GE Christmas Lighting and Decorating Guide," 1963. Reproduced with permission from GE Lighting, a business of General Electric Company.

All Is Bright: Decorating

Aluminum Trees

One legend has it that the popular 1848 engraving of Queen Victoria and her family gathered around a decorated Tannenbaum popularized Christmas trees in America. Another one traces American Christmas trees back to the holiday customs of German Hessian soldiers who had settled in Pennsylvania in the eighteenth century and fought in the Revolutionary War. Historian Stephen Nissenbaum, author of *The Battle for Christmas*, suggests that both legends are a few decades off (the Hessians are too early, Queen Victoria is too late). While the custom certainly originates in Germany, it's more likely that the wholesale adoption of holiday trees in America was actually inspired by a nineteenth-century movement in German cities that was itself a kind of folk revival, rather than the uninterrupted practice of an ancient custom. Like the nineteenth-century United States, Germany in the Victorian Age was rapidly industrializing and increasingly urban, with a growing middle class and a thriving consumer culture to go with it. Nissenbaum cites the popularity of various short stories that told of

Alcoa Aluminum newsletter, 1960. Alcoa Records, Detre Library & Archives, Senator John Heinz History Center.

the (apocryphal) custom of German children preparing and decorating trees for their parents and siblings in an admirable act of industrious selflessness. The longing for a simpler and less commercial Christmas began to appear almost as soon as the holiday itself became commercialized. Nissenbaum cites an editorial called "Reflect Before you Buy!" that appeared in a New Hampshire newspaper in 1835, warning of the holiday's focus on gifts potentially inspiring materialism and selfishness in children.

This is precisely the message of the 1965 television special *A Charlie Brown Christmas*, which, in the wholesome tradition of the Grinch, sought to teach viewers, especially young ones, that presents and glittering holiday trappings were just the symbols that represented the real holiday miracle of love and friendship. The pink, cartoon metaphor for this duality is, naturally, an aluminum Christmas tree. Aluminum trees have an outsized cultural footprint in certain parts of the United States and even enjoyed a lovingly kitschy revival of sorts with the 2004 publication of *Season's Gleamings*, a book of photographs by the artists J. Lindemann and J. Shimon, who grew up in the aluminum-producing mecca of Manitowoc, Wisconsin.

Wreath, decking, and aluminum Christmas tree, early 1960s.
Photo by Mary Evans, The Everett Collection.

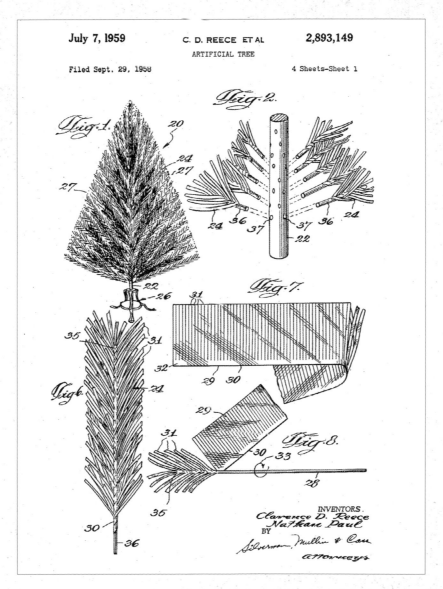

July 7, 1959   C. D. REECE ET AL   2,893,149

ARTIFICIAL TREE

Filed Sept. 29, 1958   4 Sheets—Sheet 1

Aluminum Christmas Tree Patent, 1958.

A Charlie Brown Christmas, CBS Television animated special, 1965.
Directed by Bill Melendez. Photofest, Inc.

Aluminum Christmas
trees were only popular in earnest for
a very short period, roughly 1955 through
the mid-1960s, but during that time they came to
symbolize the essence of postwar Christmas: They were
lightweight, cheery, futuristic, and fun. It's telling that of
all the different types of mass-produced holiday decorations
that proliferated in the twentieth century—the shiny glass
ornaments and the electric lights that replaced real candles,
among others—aluminum Christmas trees had the shortest
life span by far. Glass ornaments and string lights are as
popular today as they ever were. So are artificial trees in
general: Today's synthetic evergreens, meant to look
(and sometimes even smell) exactly like the real
thing, easily deceive the eye of the most
seasoned tree trimmer.

The Bob Newhart Show, "I'm Dreaming of a Slight Christmas." Featuring Bob Newhart as Bob Hartley and Marcia Wallace as Carol Kester Bondurant, November 7, 1973. Photo by CBS via Getty Images.

Midcentury Christmas

Aluminum Christmas trees for sale in the Spiegel Christmas Catalog, 1962.

All Is Bright: Decorating

99

So why was the vogue for aluminum so enthusiastic at first, and why did it vanish just as suddenly? The answer is probably that aluminum itself was so strongly correlated culturally and visually with a certain swath of postwar America; its utility and affordability made it the new wonder material of the 1950s suburbs, but this very association made it seem uncool once the 1960s counterculture was in full psychedelic swing.

If aluminum represented the Space Age, Cold War prosperity, and domestic bliss to Mom and Dad, a few years down the road the kids would naturally find it old-fashioned and far too commercial—particularly in light of the hippie movement's love for all things unprocessed and natural.

But while they sparkled and shone, aluminum Christmas trees were something to see. The concept of a metallic Christmas tree dates back at least to 1937, when *Popular Science* suggested using an insect repellent spray gun to cover an artificial flocked tree with aluminum paint.

First made by Modern Coatings in Chicago, most aluminum trees—more than one million—were produced by the Aluminum

An aluminum Christmas tree and gifts, 1964. Popperfoto/Getty Images.

All Is Bright: Decorating

A miniature aluminum Christmas tree shown with vintage Shiny Brite ornaments, both ca. late 1950s to early 1960s.
Photo by Jeffrey Stockbridge.

Print advertisements for Reynolds Metals aluminum trees and gifts, early 1960s.
Reproduced with permission from Reynolds Consumer Products.

HOW TO DECORATE YOUR NEW ALUMINUM CHRISTMAS TREE

Some Do's and Don'ts

"How to Decorate Your Aluminum Christmas Tree,"
Alcoa Aluminum, 1959. Provided by Alcoa Inc. and used
with its permission.

Before putting up your aluminum Christmas trees, check over this list of do's and don'ts to get maximum satisfaction from your purchase:

Do... assemble the tree trunk first and place it in the stand.

Do... when placing limbs into the trunk of your tree, start from the top down and place limbs carefully in holes in the trunk. Hold the limbs at the base, not in the center where you will bend the needles.

Do... use spotlights to light your tree. Special effects include rotating color wheels or rotating tree holders.

Do... decorate with glass or aluminum ornaments, preferably all the same color.

Do... use wide-mouth ornament hooks.

Do... when taking down your tree, remove ornaments carefully. Remove limbs from the top down, again holding them by the base near the trunk to protect the needles. Stored carefully in the original carton, your Alcoa aluminum tree will provide Christmas beauty in your home for years to come!

Do... remember to use *only* Underwriters' Laboratories approved electrical equipment!

Don't... tie on ornaments with string or wire that will distort needles. Use the wide-mouth hooks sold in all stores.

Don't... put tinsel, chains or streamers around aluminum trees. They clutter the inherent beauty.

Don't... display trees outdoors. Rain or snow can dull or stain the brilliant needles and destroy their beauty. If you want them seen outside, place them in a window or on a protected porch.

Proper decoration will make your aluminum tree more beautiful

An American Christmas
card featuring an aluminum
Christmas tree, 1960s.

Specialty Company in Manitowoc, Wisconsin, in the 1960s. Their most popular tree, the Evergleam, retailed for about $25. They varied in size, but generally took the same form: a wood or aluminum central pole would be drilled with holes at an angle, which would hold dozens of "branches," upon which strips of aluminum were twisted and fluffed to resemble the needles of an evergreen tree.

Because fingerprints would dull the shiny surface with oil, aluminum trees always looked best when brand-new and didn't age well. They also presented some decorating challenges: Electric lights are not safe to use on their metal branches. But this limitation led to the development of the motorized color wheel, a rotating light that shone through multicolored gels that would cast red, green, yellow and blue light across the branches of an aluminum tree.

Aluminum trees and assorted aluminum decorative products made it a point to advertise their use of Alcoa Aluminum, which, while not producing trees per se, offered advice in 1959 on how to decorate with aluminum as a DIY material and how to trim an aluminum tree.

An aluminum Christmas tree at Alcoa headquarters, 1960s. Alcoa Photographs, Detre Library & Archives, Senator John Heinz History Center.

Tinsel

Though tinsel is made from plastic today, it was actually first invented in Renaissance Germany. It dates to about 1610 in Nuremberg, and was originally fashioned from silver. Shinier metals that don't tarnish as easily were added to make early tinsel glimmer in candlelight. Starting at the turn of the twentieth century, tinsel was manufactured using aluminum, primarily in France up until World War I. After World War II, lead was used, often advertised as "fire-safe" and tarnish-proof. With increasing concern about the health effects of lead, the Food and Drug Administration banned lead tinsel in 1972, and since then it has been manufactured from either Mylar or metallic-finish polyvinyl chloride (PVC) film.

The Northern European festival of Yule is an ancestor of modern Christmas, observed in pre-Christian Germany and Scandinavia to celebrate the winter solstice. Yule has a lot in common with Roman Saturnalia, particularly in its focus on feasting, drinking, singing, and kicking back to enjoy a break from a season of hard work. Yule and "Yuletide greetings" evoke scenes of ancient

House Beautiful, December 1961. Reprinted with permission of Hearst Communications, Inc.

President Lyndon Johnson's family celebrating Christmas Eve at the White House, with a tree decorated with tinsel in the background. December 24, 1968. The Everett Collection.

Midcentury Christmas

110

coziness in a cold climate and reinforce the concept of Christmas as a back-to-basics holiday centered around home and hearth. In many Scandinavian countries today, a variation on the word "jul" refers to the Christmas holiday itself, and the greeting God Jul (literally "good Yule") means "Merry Christmas."

Like Christmas trees, edible ornaments, and wax candles, the crackling fire of imagined Yuletide feasts enjoyed a high-tech makeover in midcentury America. And It's thanks to a clever workaround solution to a programming snafu that the televised Yule log is now enjoying its own second life, streaming to a variety of holiday soundtracks on Netflix and Hulu. In November 1966, Fred M. Thrower, then general manager of WPIX in New York City, realized that the cancellation of a college basketball game

meant the station would have nothing to broadcast on Saturday, December 24, 1966. He came up with the idea of transforming televisions all over town into glowing hearths by airing four hours of cheery fireplace footage, which was shot in color at Gracie Mansion, home of then-mayor John Lindsay. The clip (it was reshot in 1970) was 17 seconds long, and there was a noticeable blip in the flames when it restarted. Thrower characterized the Yule log broadcast as a Christmas gift to both viewers and station employees. The televised Yule log would add a touch of traditional coziness to apartment dwellers who lacked a real fireplace, he reasoned, and the looping broadcast of footage would relieve WPIX staff of having to work on Christmas Eve. It went off the air in 1989, but popular demand brought it back in 2001.

CHAPTER THREE

Family lore holds that I figured out Santa's true identity sometime in the early 1980s because I was able to recognize my mother's distinctive cursive handwriting. At the time of the discovery, I vowed that if I were ever tasked with playing Santa one day, I'd learn calligraphy so that the thank-you note I left for the cookies and carrots would look appropriately antiquated. Even as a small child, I assumed that the preindustrial, old-fashioned-seeming Victorian image of Santa Claus was who he really was. I had no awareness that Santa had gone through a *Jetsons* phase.

Midcentury modern Santa Claus cut a pretty sharp figure for someone whose primary means of transportation used to be a reindeer-drawn sleigh. In the nineteenth century, the idea that Santa was making toys by hand using old-fashioned tools added a nostalgic sheen to the business of holiday retail, disguising its coarser commercial side with a patina of wholesome, preindustrial craft. The postwar obsession with outer space, both as the site of scientific exploration

Left: Advertisement for Reynolds Metals foil gift wraps, 1960s. Reproduced with permission from Reynolds Consumer Products.

Right: American Christmas Card, 1900. Art and Picture Collection, The New York Public Library Digital Collection.

Combat Operations Center at the North American Air Defense Command (NORAD), Colorado Springs, Colorado, 1950s. Bettmann/Getty Images.

Midcentury Christmas

and as the potential arena for a new kind of warfare, cast Santa's annual sleigh rides in a new light and made him an unlikely sci-fi character of sorts. Space was the place where Americans in the 1950s and '60s projected their highest hopes and their deepest anxieties. And because the night sky figures prominently in two major aspects of Christmas lore— the journey of the three wise men following the star of Bethlehem and Santa's global toy delivery—it made a certain kind of sense to weave it all together. It was probably comforting, too.

The story of how the North American Aerospace Defense Command (NORAD) began "tracking" Santa's progress across the globe on Christmas Eve, 1955, seems too good to be true, and indeed it might be, but having been relayed in the *New York Times* and confirmed by NORAD itself, it might be a genuine Christmas miracle. Legend has it that a child misdialed the number in a Sears® print ad for a Santa Claus hotline in Colorado Springs in late November and reached NORAD by accident (some versions of the story claim that the phone number in the ad was misprinted). The child allegedly reached the crew commander on duty, Colonel Harry Shoup, who was initially gruff with the caller. Shoup later came to see it as a public relations opportunity for NORAD (then called CONAD) when a member of his staff mounted a picture of Santa Claus on an aircraft tracking board as a joke. He then asked Colonel Barney Oldfield, public relations officer, to issue a press release that NORAD would "continue to track and guard Santa and his sleigh on his trip to and from the U.S. against possible attack from those who do not believe in Christmas."

Apart from being a prank that could only have occurred during the Cold War, the NORAD tradition almost sounds like a bit of *really* old-fashioned Christmas fun, like something that could happen while the Lord of Misrule presided over a rowdy banquet and costumed adults poked fun at social norms. NORAD certainly banked a bit of Christmas goodwill by showing that they were in on the joke.

Santa's foray into the world of science fiction played out in movies, on TV, and in comic books throughout the 1950s and '60s. The camp classic *Santa Claus Conquers the Martians*, which promised a glimpse at a "fantastic Martian toy factory," took the story of sci-fi Santa to the next level by offering an account of what could have happened had his space travel finally led him to another planet.

Santa's Soviet counterpart, the white-bearded Grandfather Frost, called *Ded Moroz* in Russian, also took flight, and in holiday cards from the 1960s and '70s he was depicted monitoring the progress of the rockets and satellites from the Soviet space program. In the USSR, the holiday of New Year's was a secular version of Christmas, encouraged by the state as a

kind of replacement holiday for Christmas and Hanukkah, both of which, like all religious observances, were outlawed. New Year's resembled Christmas in many ways, including the decoration of the New Year's tree, which looked for all the world like a Christmas tree with ornaments, surrounded by presents for good children delivered by Grandfather Frost on December 31. This practice eventually led to the curious custom of Soviet Jews displaying New Year's trees in their homes, to the bafflement of their new neighbors when they began emigrating to Israel and the United States in the 1970s and '80s.

New Year's card from the USSR, ca. 1960s–1970s.

Poster advertising *Santa Claus Conquers the Martians*,
Embassy Pictures Corporation, 1964.

onica Pidgeon

Alfo Lasty

EETINGS

from the
editors of

CHITECTU

1960

Greeting Cards

Midcentury Christmas cards featured a dizzying array of images, some of which were cozy evocations of an old-fashioned Victorian Christmas, while others radiated pure Atomic Age kitsch. And the creations of professional designers like Robert Brownjohn, Henry Dreyfuss, Charles and Ray Eames, Theo Crosby, and *New York Times* circulation chief Nat W. Goldstein took the path-breaking graphic sensibility of the postwar design world and fused it with the playful spirit of Christmas.

The practice of sending greeting cards is quite ancient, with handmade versions dating as far back as ancient Egypt and China, particularly around the New Year's holiday. In the Renaissance, hand-printed cards for Valentine's Day and New Year's Day were popular, though relatively costly.

This Holiday season . . .

Left: Christmas card from Monica Pigeon, Theo Crosby, and the editors of *Architectural Design* to Charles and Ray Eames, ca. 1950s. Library of Congress Prints and Photographs Division, Washington, DC. Reproduced by permission of the Crosby Estate and the Theo Crosby Archive at the University of Brighton Design Archives.

Right: Christmas card, "This Holiday Season." 1957, USA. Cooper Hewitt, Smithsonian Design Museum/Art Resource, New York.

Left: Robert Brownjohn, Donna, Eliza, and Robert Christmas card, lithograph, late 1950s.

Right: Robert Brownjohn, Masterset Brushes, Inc. Christmas card, lithograph and cotton, late 1950s.

Gifts of Don Goeman. © The Estate of Robert Brownjohn. Images © The Museum of Modern Art/Licensed by SCALA/Art Resource, New York.

The rise of mass-produced printed cards in the mid-nineteenth century transformed them into an accessible luxury. In 1843, industrialist Henry Cole, a founder of the Victoria and Albert Museum, commissioned illustrator John Callcott Horsley to design the first known Christmas card, which he mailed out to his circle of friends. German immigrant Louis Prang is sometimes called the father of the American greeting card, having popularized them in the United States during the 1870s, using cutting-edge chromolithography techniques he learned in Germany.

The most widely recognized name in any kind of greeting card is Hallmark. Founded in 1910 by businessman Joyce Hall, who saw opportunity in the postcard craze of 1903 while working in his family's general store in Nebraska, Hallmark Cards remains the largest producer of greeting cards in the United States. Hallmark began selling Valentine's Day and Christmas cards under the name Hall Brothers, and during the 1920s and '30s they expanded to produce wrapping paper and cards for a wide array of holidays and occasions, adopting the name "Hallmark" in 1928.

Leading figures in the postwar design world, for all their seriousness about modernism, sent each other cheery cards that would be a delight to find in the mail even now. Charles and Ray Eames were both copious letter writers, and their holiday cards often featured images of themselves in funny poses. A selection of their cards from the 1940s shows them variously reflected in a glass Christmas ball, floating inside a Christmas ball in miniature, and dangling ornaments against the backdrop of a modern sculpture. On the reverse sides, Ray's charming handwriting and drawings accompany the couple's greetings. Graphic designer Robert Brownjohn, whose Christmas ball sculpture adorned the lobby of Pepsi-Cola headquarters in 1958, created graphic Christmas cards both for his own family and for corporate clients. A stylized Christmas stocking features a circular photograph of his infant daughter Eliza from the late 1950s, and another from the same period designed for Masterset Brushes, Inc. shows the top of Santa's red cap peeking out of a white brick chimney.

Henry Dreyfuss, whose iconic designs include the Hoover Model 65 convertible vacuum cleaner, the Westclox Big Ben alarm clock, and the Princess telephone, sent holiday cards to friends, notably Charles and Ray Eames. His 1945 card shows what appears to be a red-nosed reindeer, only to reveal when unfolded an extra-long dachshund with the word "greetings" written across his body. His tail supports a sign, tied with red ribbon, which reads: "From all the Dreyfusses." And interior designer William Pahlmann drew and collaged whimsical cards by hand, even dreaming up two "concept trees" in 1955 for the Fine Arts Group of Southern California Assistance League, which asked prominent designers to submit holiday decorating ideas for its annual fund-raiser.

Henry Dreyfuss, Christmas card from "the Dreyfusses" to Charles and Ray Eames, ca. 1950s. Library of Congress Prints and Photographs Division, Washington, DC. Reproduced with permission of the estate of Henry Dreyfuss.

Opposite: American Christmas card, 1960s.

Space Age cards for the mass market, both from major producers like Hallmark and smaller companies that have since folded, featured a mixture of old-fashioned scenes and very of-the-moment depictions of a rocket-powered Santa or atomic-style trees and ornaments. One foldout card from the early 1960s depicts Santa Claus flying a rocket loaded with toys and decorated with Christmas tree and snowflake stencils on the exterior. The card itself folds out into a paper template that can be cut and folded to create "your own spaceship," essentially a Santa Flier or fancy paper airplane. A similar card shows Santa with two elves, dressed in red suits and overalls, holding tools and pointing to a blueprint of a streamlined sleigh. Though their aprons and toolbox look quite old-fashioned, their pose echoes countless photographs of NASA engineers at work from the 1950s and '60s. And where Santa isn't present, trees and toys usually are. One especially vibrant card from the late 1950s shows three Christmas trees, two of which appear to be artificial—one flocked and one aluminum. All three have tree stands with tiny balls at the end of each leg, making them resemble a model of the atom. The ornaments are classic bauble shapes, with a few birds and bells, and the evergreen tree in the center has a Sputnik-style tree-topper.

Season's Greetings FROM EPICURE KITCHENS, INC. AIRLINE PURVEYORS AND FOOD CONSULTANTS

Top: Henry Dreyfuss, Christmas card from "the Dreyfusses" to Charles and Ray Eames, ca. 1950s.
Library of Congress Prints and Photographs Division, Washington, DC. Reproduced with
permission of the estate of Henry Dreyfuss.

Bottom: Robert Brownjohn, Epicure Kitchens Christmas card, lithograph, late 1950s. Gift of Don Goeman. © The Estate of
Robert Brownjohn. Image © The Museum of Modern Art/Licensed by SCALA/Art Resource, New York.

Christmas card (photograph) from Charles and Ray Eames showing them reflected in a mercury glass Christmas ornament, December, 1941. Image © 2016 Eames Office, LLC (eamesoffice.com).

Christmas 1946

much love to you
mother – it was
wonderful to have
our visit this fall.
Charlie (or Ray)

AND LOVE AND MERRY CHRISTMAS
WISHES FROM RAY.
WE ARE SENDING YOU A CHAIR
WHICH WILL BE LATE! xxx

Above: Christmas card (photograph) from Charles and Ray Eames showing them waving from inside an ornament or snow globe, December 1946. Library of Congress Prints and Photographs Division, Washington, DC. Image © 2016 Eames Office, LLC (eamesoffice.com).

Opposite: Christmas card (photograph) from Charles and Ray Eames showing Ray holding an ornament with an abstract sculpture behind herself and Charles, December 1942. Image © 2016 Eames Office, LLC (eamesoffice.com).

Gifts & Greetings

Christmas card (photograph) from Charles and Ray Eames showing them flying among birds and ornaments, December 1947. Library of Congress Prints and Photographs Division, Washington, DC. Image © 2016 Eames Office, LLC (eamesoffice.com).

Greetings!

Bill Pahlmann

Left: William Pahlmann Christmas card, mid-1950s. William Pahlmann Associates Records, Hagley Museum and Library.

Below: William Pahlmann, leather Christmas tree sketch for the Christmas tree at the Fine Arts Group of Southern California Assistance League, 1955. William Pahlmann Associates Records, Hagley Museum and Library.

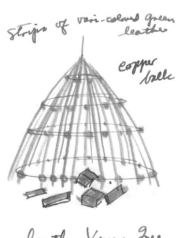

strips of vari-colored green leather

copper balls

leather Xmas tree
inside completely filled with copper wrapped packages.

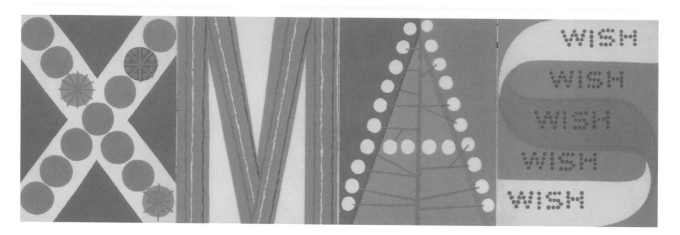

Top: Frederick Hammersley Christmas card to an unidentified recipient, ca. 1952-53.
Frederick Hammersley papers, Archives of American Art, Smithsonian Institution.

Bottom: American Christmas card, 1950s and 1960s.

Midcentury Christmas

American Christmas cards, 1950s and 1960s.

A BOOK OF CHRISTMAS QUIPS FOR YOU

American Christmas cards, 1960s.

Christmas Greetings

American Christmas cards, 1950s and 1960s.

Gifts & Greetings

TO WISH YOU

American Christmas cards, 1950s and 1960s.

Midcentury Christmas

American Christmas card, gold stamp on paper, 1957. Gift of Richard P. Wunder.
Cooper Hewitt, Smithsonian Design Museum/Art Resource, New York.

Gifts & Greetings

Shopping

One of the most beloved Christmas movies of all time, *Miracle on 34th Street*, takes place in Santa's home away from the North Pole: an American department store.

The plot of the movie is classically postwar American in that its finale features the formation of a new family that moves into a large suburban house. Santa Claus is the character who helps make this happen, fulfilling the wish of Susan, the daughter of single mom and successful Macy's events director Doris Walker (played by Maureen O'Hara). Susan tells Kris Kringle, as he's referred to in the film, that she wants a real house, not just a doll's house. She doesn't want to live in a Manhattan apartment with her mother; she'd prefer a childhood in the

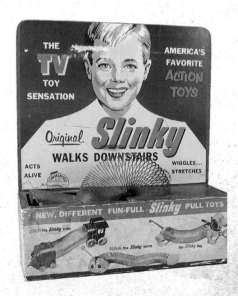

Opposite: A man loaded with gifts enters the subway at 34th Street, the stop nearest to Macy's department store in New York City, 1960. Phil Greitzer/*New York Daily News* via Getty Images.

Right: Slinky, 1956, James Industries, Inc. The Strong National Museum of Play. Image courtesy of The Strong, Rochester, New York.

country with a mom and a
dad. And in the end she gets it because her
mother and their neighbor, Fred Gailey, fall in
love. Kris Kringle is, of course, the real Santa Claus in
the movie, with a real beard that doesn't come off and an
uncanny command of any language spoken by a child waiting
in line to see him. The gag of the film, that Kris is the "real
thing," demonstrates how pervasive department store Santas
were and to what lengths stores would go to fashion magical
settings for them in their toy departments. Marshall Field's in
Chicago, Macy's in New York City, Gimbels in Philadelphia,
and countless other stores across the United States created
temporary "villages" with elves, sparkly decorations,
music, and costumed staffers. Wanamaker's in
Philadelphia was famous for its

Poster advertising *Miracle on 34th Street*, 1947. Directed by George Seaton, featuring Maureen O'Hara as Doris Walker and John Payne as Fred Gailey. Photofest, Inc.

Gifts & Greetings

SEARS

Christmas Book

1958

SHOP SEARS EASY TELEPHONE WAY
For numbers to call see pages 260 to 263
Index starts on Page 257   Easy Terms on Page 264

ORNAMENTS SHOWN ARE SOLD ON PAGE 336

SEARS, ROEBUCK AND CO., PHILADELPHIA 32, PA.
SATISFACTION GUARANTEED OR YOUR MONEY BACK

Opposite: A Christmas catalog from Macy's department store, New York City, 1940s.

Left: The Sears® Christmas "Wish Book," 1958.

Christmas display at Marshall Field & Company, Chicago, Illinois, 1956.
Reproduced with permission from Macy's.

Midcentury Christmas

144

monorail, which circled the toy department on the eighth floor from 1946–84.
Designers at Marshall Field's in the late
1940s created a display called the "Cozy
Cloud Cottage," which resembled a
modernist house in California or South
Florida, complete with sliding screen
doors, white brick, and a flat roof, all
decked out with ribbon and ornaments.

Before the advent of online shopping,
wistful Americans could "window-shop"
at home thanks to magazines and catalogs.
The Sears® Christmas "Wish Book,"
which first appeared in 1933, was a much-
anticipated visual feast of gifts and toys,
almost encyclopedic in its scope. It was
also an arbiter of style: The 1958 edition
featured a close-up of a white-flocked
artificial tree decorated with shiny,
pastel-colored ornaments.

Two employees of Pan American Airways in the toy department of Macy's
department store in New York City at Christmas during their world trip,
a journey of 26,000 miles in twenty-five days. *Picture Post*, December
1954. *Picture Post*/Hulton Archive/Getty Images.

Wrapping Paper

Like greeting cards, wrapping paper has a surprisingly long history that dates back to ancient China. Paper was invented in China in the second century B.C., and the custom of wrapping gifts of money emerged among court officials during the Southern Song Dynasty (1127–1279). The Japanese custom of *furoshiki*, in which silk or cotton fabric would be elegantly wrapped around a gift, dates from the Edo period (1603–1868) and is enjoying a revival today, thanks to its eco-friendliness. Well-heeled Europeans used expensive, hand-decorated paper to wrap their gifts starting in the nineteenth century, but more flexible tissue paper in bright colors became more popular in the twentieth century.

The origin of the modern wrapping paper industry can be traced back to Hallmark. The

HOLIDAY GREETINGS

Left and Right: American gift wrap, 1950s and 1960s.

Hall Brothers were enjoying an exceptionally busy Christmas season in December 1917 and ran out of their standard tissue paper, leaving them to use fancier printed paper as a temporary workaround. They sold it for ten cents per sheet. This turned out to be a huge hit with shoppers, who asked for it the following year. In 1919, the Halls decided to try selling their own printed paper for different occasions, just like their cards, and commercial wrapping paper has been popular ever since. Midcentury wrapping paper tended to mimic the printed textiles of the era. Unlike cards, which feature one or two images, wrapping paper "repeats," like wallpaper or upholstery fabric, so small patterns that look good in multiples lend themselves well to wrapping paper designs. Recognizable images of Santa, holly, candles, or gifts were popular, as were Christmas balls and trees.

Right: *Popular Mechanics Christmas Handbook*, 1952. Reprinted with permission of Hearst Communications.

Opposite: American gift wrap, 1950s and 1960s.

Gift-Wrapping MAGIC

IT'S WHAT'S in the gift package that counts, to be sure, but there's no getting away from it—the wrapping creates the first impression. Nothing will take the edge off lively anticipation so much as a messy, hard-to-undo package.

The first step in thoughtful holiday gift wrapping lies in the correct selection of paper and ribbon. The size and shape of the package and the taste of the recipient should be carefully considered. Large patterns are available for large packages, small designs for the little parcels. Frequently a part of a large pattern is perfect for a spe-

cific small package. All that is required then is to center the paper properly on the face of the package so just the desired part of the design is highlighted. The bow should then be placed on the package so that it does not cover the design and ruin the desired effect. Diagonal patterns and stripes are especially good for round boxes. All-over repeat patterns allow for a bow almost anywhere, but pictorial designs should be left to show, with a bow off to one side. Appropriate designs in wrapping paper should be selected to suit the recipient's taste, whether it be masculine or feminine,

146

Left: Wrapping paper, "Star of Bethlehem," ca. 1940-59, USA. Print on paper. Gift of Christopher and Esther Pullman. Cooper Hewitt, Smithsonian Design Museum/Art Resource, New York.

Right: American gift wrap, 1950s and 1960s.

Opposite: Wrapping paper, "Christmas Trees," ca. 1940-59, made by the Crystal Tissue Company. Print on paper. Gift of Christopher and Esther Pullman. Cooper Hewitt, Smithsonian Design Museum/Art Resource, New York.

American gift wrap, 1950s and 1960s.

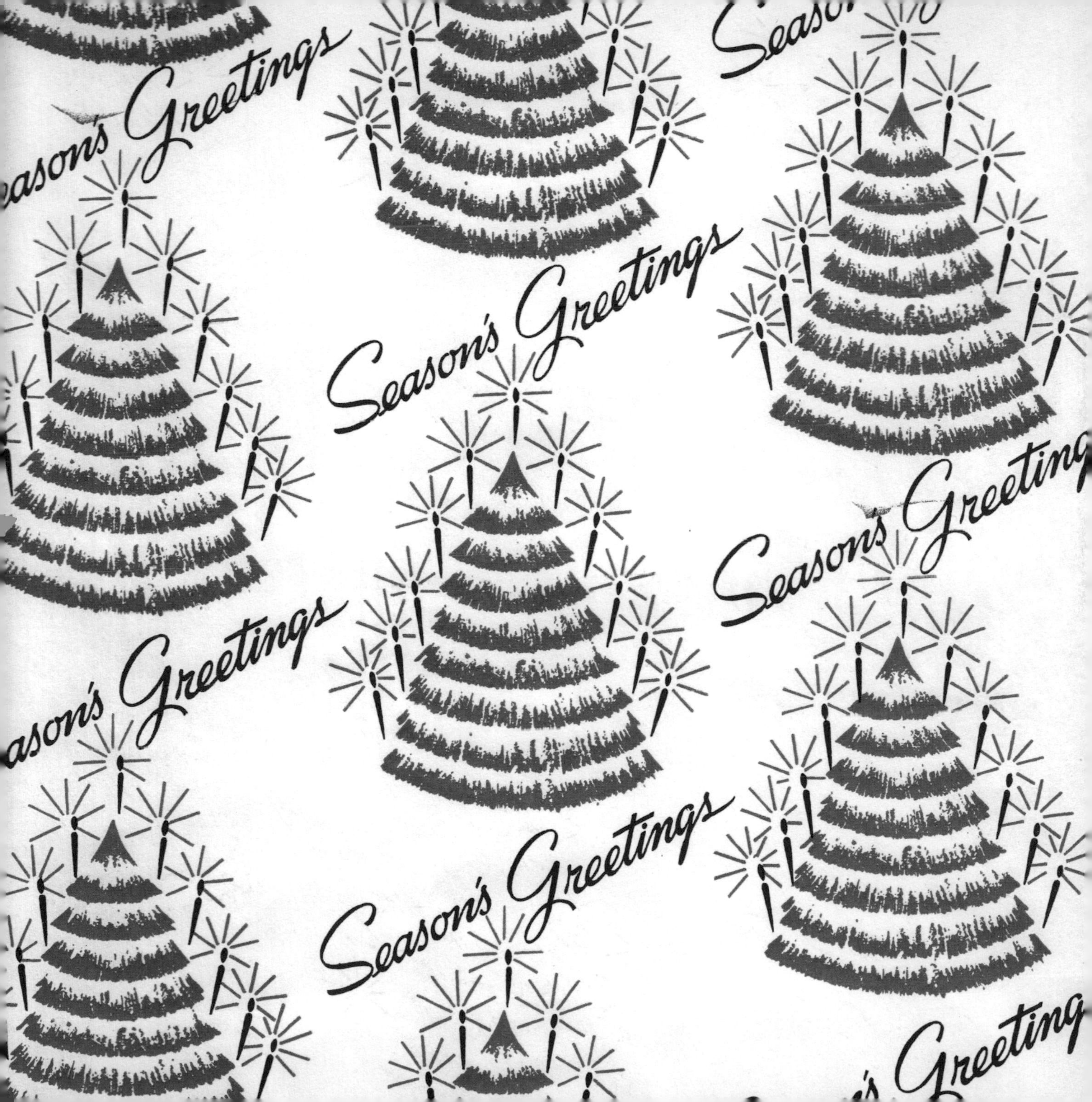
Season's Greetings
Season's Greetings
Season's Greetings

Toys

Toys in the postwar period were more colorful, dynamic, heavily marketed, and gender specific than ever before. It's also probably fair to say they were more fun than ever, too. Toys have long served as a kind of mirror version of the adult world, offering children a way to play at adulthood, trying out miniature versions of the everyday objects that form the adult world. Tiny stoves, domestic appliances and tea sets; dolls; dollhouses; and doll clothes; chemistry and erector sets; little cars; telescopes; microscopes; and art supplies of all sorts let kids try certain aspects of adulthood on for size, and in the 1950s and '60s, if toys are any indication, the toy-making adults of the world focused their attentions on science, technology, domesticity, and fashion. The postwar period made playtime look like a pint-sized mock-up of *House Beautiful* crossed with *Scientific American*: Little boys were encouraged to play scientist and engineer, and little girls were enticed by colorful working appliances or a chicly outfitted Barbie. Certain toys had crossover appeal, like Silly Putty, the Slinky, Etch A Sketch, Spirograph, and the perennial cozy stuffed animals.

A boy watches a demonstration of a Slinky "walking" down steps, 1946. Bettmann/Getty Images.

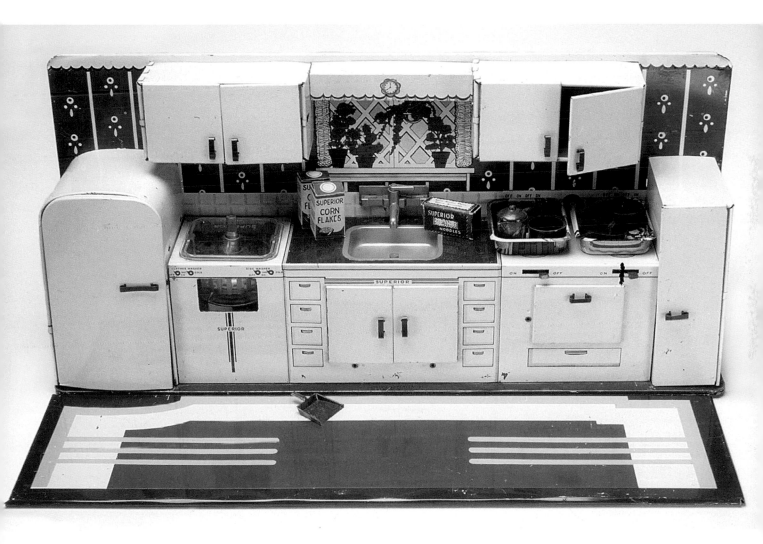

Superior Kitchen, T. Cohn Inc., New York City, 1950s. The Strong National Museum of Play.
Image courtesy of The Strong, Rochester, New York.

Opposite: A young girl sits and speaks on a toy telephone, holding a Raggedy Ann doll near her play kitchen, 1955.
Harold M. Lambert/Lambert/Getty Images.

Silly Putty owes its life to wartime rationing, which inspired researchers to experiment with synthetic alternatives to natural rubber. Its invention has been credited to numerous scientists, and it's not clear who was first: Earl Warrick of Dow Corning or James Wright of General Electric. In 1943, both scientists and their teams independently realized that combining boric acid with silicone oil yielded a bouncy, elastic material that had many of the properties of rubber, but didn't quite work as a replacement for it. Marketing consultant Peter Hodgson worked with toy shop owner Ruth Fallgatter to try to market the putty in 1949, with modest results. The following year, Hodgson redesigned the packaging, naming the substance Silly Putty and packaging it in red plastic eggs. Silly Putty got off to a slow start, enjoying a temporary boost in sales thanks to a mention in *The New Yorker*, though the Korean War slowed production because a key ingredient, silicone, was rationed. In 1957, Hodgson made the first TV commercial for Silly Putty, airing during *The Howdy Doody Show*. By 1961, Silly Putty was sold around the world and even became popular in Europe and the Soviet Union. In 1968, a Silly Putty egg orbited the moon,

Etch A Sketch, Ohio Art Co., 1960. The Strong National Museum of Play. Gift of Robert and Doris Zabel in memory of their grandson, Seth White. Image courtesy of The Strong, Rochester, New York.

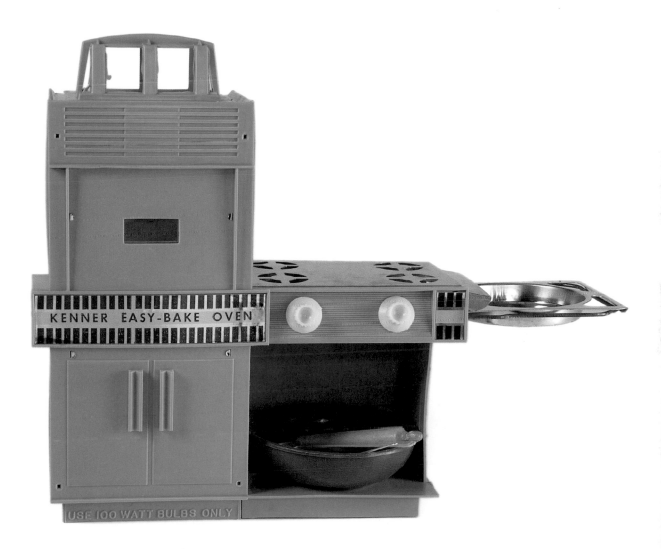

Opposite and above: Easy-Bake Oven, Kenner Products Co., 1964.
The Strong National Museum of Play. Image courtesy of The Strong, Rochester, New York.

Gifts & Greetings

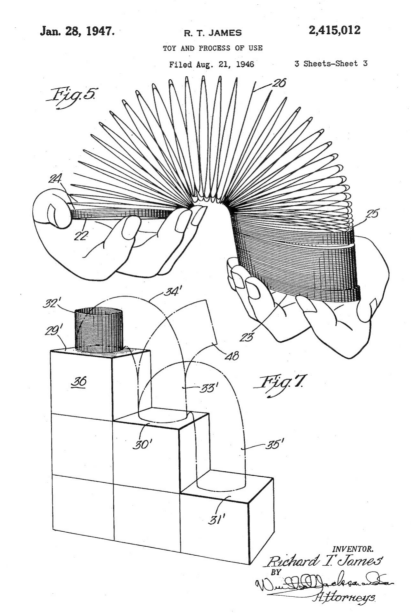

Jan. 28, 1947.

R. T. JAMES

2,415,012

TOY AND PROCESS OF USE

Filed Aug. 21, 1946

3 Sheets–Sheet 3

Fig.5.

26

24

22

25

23

32'

34'

29'

36

48

30'

33'

35'

31'

Fig.7.

INVENTOR.
Richard T. James
BY
Wm. Jackson
Attorneys.

Patent for the Slinky, filed
January 28, 1947, by
Richard T. James, James
Industries, Upper Darby,
Pennsylvania.

Midcentury Christmas

brought along for the ride by the Apollo 8 astronauts.

The Slinky was invented in 1943 by a naval engineer named Richard T. James and first demonstrated to the public at Gimbels Department Store in Philadelphia in 1945. James was stationed at a shipyard in Philadelphia during the war, and he was working on the development of springs that could be used to stabilize ships carrying sensitive equipment in choppy waters. Accidentally knocking a spring off his worktable, he was intrigued to find that the spring appeared to "step" as though it was walking down a flight of stairs over a stack of books and onto the floor. He experimented with different sizes and shapes of steel wire, eventually fabricating a spring that could "walk," to the fascination of neighborhood children. James's wife Betty named the toy "Slinky," finding it in the dictionary and deciding that the word evoked the sound of the spring "walking." The first demonstration at Gimbels made use of an inclined plane. The following year, in 1946, the Slinky premiered at the American Toy Fair. Like Silly Putty, the Slinky was heavily promoted in commercials and print ads aimed at children, but it also had (and continues to have) a cult following among adults. Slinkys are frequently used as math and physics teaching tools, and they have been pressed into service at NASA for experiments too.

Just at the moment when real appliances were starting to appear in bright colors to coordinate with stylish American kitchens, the iconic Easy-Bake Oven appeared, offering little girls a taste of postwar domestic bliss. The first Easy-Bake was produced by Kenner in 1963, and in that year alone more than 500,000 were sold. Though contemporary versions of the Easy-Bake Oven are styled differently (they resemble microwave ovens today and are produced by Hasbro), the essential elements haven't changed:

The oven is sold with packets of cake mix, round pans, and a light bulb that heats and bakes the miniature cakes. Easy-Bake Ovens originally had 100-watt bulbs as their heating elements and came in pale yellow or turquoise, mirroring the fashionable hues of the era. As the sixties progressed, the color palette changed, and by 1969 the "Premier" line of ovens came in avocado green and deep red.

My memories of Barbie are mostly concerned with her hair: At some point in the mid-1980s, I got my hands on a Conair hair crimper, which came with a zigzag crimping iron designed to emulate the most au courant hairstyles. I had more latitude to use the crimper on Barbie's hair than my own and, alas, it didn't fare too well. Still, Barbie was always chic and somehow seemed pulled together, even in nonstandard outfits or with experimental '80s hair. That's no accident: She was the first American doll specifically designed for kids to look like an adult.

When Barbie was first introduced in 1959 wearing a zebra-striped swimsuit, no one knew that she would amass a worldwide following, scores of outfits, a car, or a Dream House, but in retrospect, it seems inevitable. Barbie's creator, Ruth Handler, observed her daughter Barbara playing with paper dolls and noticed that she enjoyed giving them adult identities, yet most dolls during this period were modeled on babies and children, meant to be cared for rather than looked up to. The idea of a grown-up "role-model" doll was new, and Mattel executives were initially unimpressed by the idea. Handler created Barbie in 1956, using a German doll called Bild Lilli as a template. Bild Lilli was based on a newspaper comic character, and she was portrayed as a professional, beautiful woman who was independent and witty. Bild Lilli was originally marketed (oddly enough) to adults, but her array of fashionable outfits made her an instant and unexpected hit with kids, and herein lay Barbie's appeal some years later. Mattel would

The millionth Barbie sold in Germany, 1965. Ullstein Bild via Getty Images.

Barbie's Dream House, Mattel, Inc., Hawthorne, California, 1962–65.
The Strong National Museum of Play. Image courtesy of The Strong, Rochester, New York.

Midcentury Christmas

later buy the rights to Bild Lilli, which stopped production in 1964, and Barbie's empire went global. She was initially marketed as a "Teen-age Fashion Model" (the single word "teenage" was not yet common in popular speech). Around 350,000 Barbie dolls were sold during the first year of production.

Barbie was one of the first toys in the world to benefit from extensive advertising on television, which has since become a de rigueur practice for the toy industry. Current estimates place the total number of Barbies sold worldwide at more than 1 billion in more than 150 countries. Barbie's toy landscape reflected much about the postwar world and the evolving role of women during that period, and indeed Barbie "trying on" various professional identities, like stewardess or fashion model, captured something in the experience of real American women who were making forays into the working world of the 1960s without many female role models to draw from. Barbie's world of dream homes, cars, boyfriend Ken, and her flair for fashion speaks volumes about the complex position of the successful single American woman in the very early days of feminism. Despite being happy and independent, she is still judged on her outward appearance and her clothes.

Don Herbert as Mr. Wizard with "Christmas crystals" in 1959.
Photo by Frank Carroll/NBC Universal Photo Bank via Getty Images.

Gilbert Chemistry Experiment Lab No. 12055, manufactured by A. C. Gilbert Company, New Haven, Connecticut, 1950s. Chemical Heritage Foundation collections, photo by Gregory Tobias. Courtesy of the Chemical Heritage Foundation.

Above: Chemcraft Chemistry Lab featuring Atomic Energy, manufactured by Porter Chemical Company, Hagerstown, Maryland, 1950s. Chemical Heritage Foundation collections, photo by Gregory Tobias. Courtesy of the Chemical Heritage Foundation.

Right: Chemcraft Chemistry Lab, manufactured by Lionel-Porter, Hagerstown, Maryland, 1950s. Chemical Heritage Foundation collections, photo by Gregory Tobias. Courtesy of the Chemical Heritage Foundation.

Chemistry sets are among the oldest of "modern" toys, with their origins in the seventeenth- and eighteenth-century fascination with minerals and metals. Chemists, pharmacists, and medical students had portable chemistry sets that could be used in the field, and wealthy people (of both sexes) with an interest in science purchased elaborate kits of various types. Somewhere in between a toy and a hobby, such kits were the ancestors of the modern chemistry set, which, like toy microscopes and telescopes, was designed to inspire scientific curiosity in children—generally boys. The earliest commercial chemistry sets were manufactured in the United States mainly by the Porter Chemical Company under the "Chemcraft" trademark, and by the A. C. Gilbert Company, which introduced pink chemistry sets in the 1950s that encouraged girls to become "laboratory assistants" rather than chemists in their own right. Through the 1950s, sets like the Atomic Energy Lab included real radioactive ore, which was subsequently eliminated, along with some other chemicals, due to rising safety concerns in the 1960s.

Well before the moon landing in 1969, the lure of outer space, strange planets, aliens, and futuristic ray guns captured the American imagination, and a whole new category of toys took flight. In the 1930s, science-fiction comic books and radio programs popularized characters like Buck Rogers and Flash Gordon, inspiring early "ray guns" like the Flash Gordon Radio Repeater (made from tin) and stylized action figures. After Word War II, Japan began to produce robots, often with outer space or atomic themes, including Mr. Atomic. The *Tom Corbett, Space Cadet* TV series (popular in the 1950s), *Star Trek*, and, of course, NASA itself inspired the production of toy space capsules and rockets, made all the more exciting on July 21, 1969, when kids could watch as astronaut Neil Armstrong became the first human being to set foot on the moon.

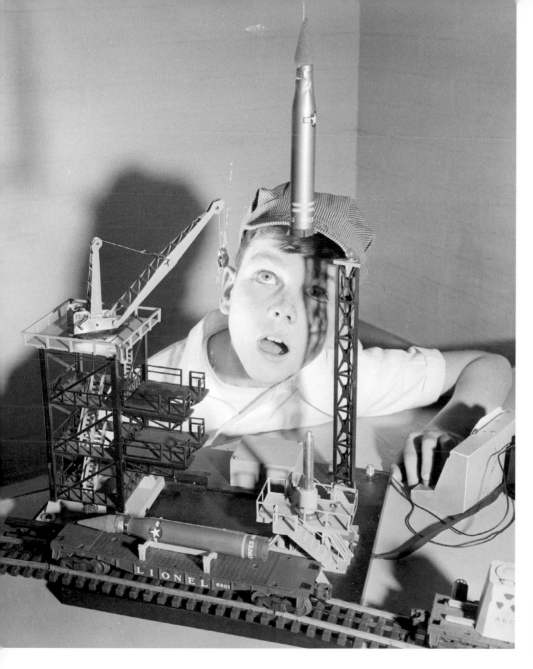

Danny Gray presses a button on a
Lionel rocket launcher at the Toy
Guidance Council, New York City,
1958. Bettmann/Getty Images.

Gifts & Greetings

Glenn Sitterly, four years old, demonstrates his space suit and disintegrator pistol on a rocket ship ride at the American Toy Fair, New York, 1953. Bettmann/Getty Images.

Left: Macy's department store featuring space toys on the shelves, New York, 1957. Ted Russell/The *LIFE* Images Collection/Getty Images.

Right: German-born American rocket scientist Wernher von Braun with U.S. President John F. Kennedy touring Cape Canaveral, Florida, November 16, 1963. NASA/Interim Archives/Getty Images.

Gifts & Greetings

Opposite: *The New Yorker*, "Space Toys for Christmas" cover illustration by Anatol Kovarsky, December 9, 1961. © Condé Nast.

Mars rocket toy, Masudaya, Tokyo, Japan, 1950. The Strong National Museum of Play.
Image courtesy of The Strong, Rochester, New York.

Grown-Up Gifts

Before Christmas was reconceived as a family-friendly holiday that centered around children, gifts tended to run to adult tastes for things like books, clothes, fine food, jewelry, and other keepsakes.

But postwar grown-ups got to play house just like their kids in the 1950s and '60s, when it seemed that everything from a new stove to a washer-dryer to a sleek, red typewriter—at least, as far as advertisers were concerned—was as exciting and fun as a new toy. Santa Claus himself, or more specifically his office workflow, advertised the new IBM Dictaphone in a 1966 print ad. "With this 28 ounce unit," Santa says, "I don't have to trust important things to memory, like who gets a football. And who gets a diamond necklace." IBM advertised its office machines more generally in a colorful ad featuring a mod, stylized tableau of gifts with the tagline: "Ever find IBM under your Christmas tree?"

Gene Kelly and Fred Astaire dance together on a Christmas-themed set with wrapped presents and stuffed animals during a photo shoot for *LIFE* magazine, 1958. J. R. Eyerman/ The *LIFE* Picture Collection/Getty Images.

Other companies relied on the lure of color to sell evergreen products like furniture and appliances. The General Telephone System told consumers to "Give Color" in a December 1957 print ad in which a bright red Model 500 Telephone, designed by Henry Dreyfuss, is held up as a perfect holiday gift. Cosco Metal Furniture presented an array of affordable card tables, playpens, serving carts, room dividers, and chairs, styled with holly and evergreen branches, and displayed by a model sporting a Mrs. Claus-style red dress with white fur trim. Santa Claus appeared to spring from a jack-in-the-box holding a blue Smith Corona typewriter in a colorful print ad from 1955. And for GE and Westinghouse, major manufacturers of appliances and kitchen gadgets, Santa was portrayed as the harbinger of domestic bliss. A print ad that appeared in *The Saturday Evening Post* in the late 1950s declared: "Santa Claus and Westinghouse are in cahoots!" and noted that their appliances, like automatic coffeemakers and pop-up toasters, "say 'Merry Christmas' 365 days a year."

Throughout the 1950s and '60s, GE advertised its array of products for both inside and outside the home, from portable

Advertisement for IBM, 1966. Reprint Courtesy of International Business Machines Corporation, © International Business Machines Corporation.

Advertisement for Cosco Metal Furniture, 1958. Reproduced with permission from Ameriwood Industries, Inc. DBA Cosco Home and Office Products.

Gifts & Greetings

Santa Claus and Westinghouse Are in Cahoots!

Take a tip from Santa . . . these grand Westinghouse Appliances are what everybody wants

Once in a blue moon, the *perfect* Christmas Gift comes along . . . a gift you love to give and folks love to receive. Here is a wide variety of such gifts . . . the big, famous family of Westinghouse Gift Appliances. They're glamorous to look at . . . still more glamorous to use . . . and so varied they'll put stars in the eyes of everyone on your list.

Take the Roaster, for instance, that cooks everything, plugs in anywhere. With it you give easier, better cooking to any homemaker you know.

Electric Bed Coverings . . . Comforter, Sheet or Blanket . . . mean warmth—without—weight . . . perfect sleep the whole night through. With the Automatic Coffee Maker and Pop-Up Toaster you'll give delicious, easy-to-get breakfasts.

The new square Waffle Baker brings along wonderful Sunday night suppers and luncheon treats. You'll give freedom from fatigue with the Irons, and easier, more successful cooking with the powerful Mixer that whips up almost any food without changing speeds. Every member of the family will say "thanks a million" when they see how the new Electric Griddle broils 10 whopping hamburgers at a time . . . fries, grills, toasts foods to perfection, too.

See these and a dozen more practical, welcome Westinghouse Appliances at your retailer's now. There are gifts for every taste and budget. This year, give *Lifts to Living* to everyone. The Westinghouse Electric Corporation, Electric Appliance Division, Mansfield, Ohio.

See TV's Top Dramatic Show . . . "Westinghouse STUDIO ONE" . . . Every Week

YOU CAN BE SURE .. IF IT's Westinghouse

GIFTS THAT SAY
"Merry Christmas"
365 DAYS A YEAR

ROASTER-OVEN, America's favorite. Two square feet of cooking magic.

SQUARE WAFFLE BAKER cooks 4 large waffles, just as you like them, automatically.

ELECTRIC GRIDDLE, generous capacity for frying, grilling, toasting.

AUTOMATIC COFFEE MAKER for perfect coffee every time. Keeps it hot. Holds 8 cups.

POP-UP TOASTER makes toast exactly as you want it, automatically. Has push-up lever.

ELECTRIC BED COVERINGS, Comforter, Sheet or Blanket. Automatic warmth - without - weight.

ADJUST-O-MATIC SANDWICH GRILL toasts, fries, grills. Has automatic Heat Control.

STREAMLINER IRON, Fabric Dial has 3 speeds for each different fabric. Safety signal light.

ADJUST-O-MATIC IRON has Fabric Selector Dial, easy-grip handle. Heats rapidly.

MIXER, so powerful . . . needs only one speed setting for most recipes. Juicer optional.

 Exhaust Fan   Hand Vac   Electric Sheet   Hot Plate   Warming Pad   Dishwasher   Laundromat   Dryer   Refrigerator   Home Freezer   Range   Water Heater   Percolator   Electric Comforter

Advertisement for Westinghouse, 1950s. Reproduced with permission from CBS Corporation.

Santa's favorite cigar

Paul Rand illustration for
El Producto Cigars, "Santa's
Favorite Cigar," offset lithograph
on paper, 1953-57. Cooper
Hewitt, Smithsonian Design
Museum/Art Resource,
New York. Photo by Matt Flynn.

Gifts & Greetings

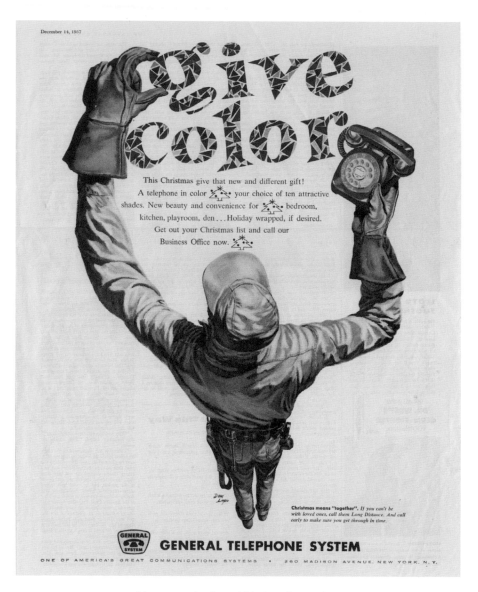

Advertisement for General Telephone System, 1957.

hair dryers and television sets in fashionable colors to waffle irons and strings of electric lights for holiday decor. Though the company was strongly associated with particular kinds of goods, particularly lightbulbs, GE made an effort in its advertising to promote the ideas of technology and newness as its own signature selling point, knowing that the gadgets of any particular holiday season would be nearly obsolete a few years later. In one double-page ad from the mid-1960s promoting portable TVs, the tagline read: "Progress is our most important product."

Print advertisement for a General Electric portable television set, 1960s. Reproduced with permission from GE Lighting, a business of General Electric Company.

Gifts & Greetings

ow in handsome colors: the Olivetti
ttera 22, the _portable_ portable. Travel-
g companion, family friend, student's
light, it provides all the important
atures of big standard typewriters.
ue, green or gray, $88 plus tax.

olivetti

he Olivetti Studio 44 is a somewhat
rger portable, with the feel and features
a standard; type on it blindfolded
d we think you'll mistake it for one.
ue or gray, $115 plus tax. Olivetti,
0 Fifth Avenue, New York 36, N. Y.

ever find
IBM
under your
Christmas
Tree?

If you've
under yo
for a mer
might thi
But it's
shops an
data pro
ture and
the other
holiday
Yes . .
helps ad
speeds th
merry Ch

IB

wondered how the good things
were made and delivered in time
stmas morning, the last thing you
a battery of busy IBM machines.
in thousands of bustling work-
es throughout the world, IBM
systems help in the manufac-
ution of toys and clothes and all
erful things that enter into your

y day, in uncounted ways, IBM
e pleasure of daily living . . .
ress that makes for many, many
ses!

DATA
PROCESSING

DATA PROCESSING
ELECTRIC TYPEWRITE
MILITARY PRODUCTS
TIME EQUIPMENT

Surprise the family
with the most useful gift of all

Smith-Corona
the world's finest
and fastest portable

Five models to choose from . . .
Silent-Super in four outstanding
colors: Alpine Blue, Desert Sand,
Seafoam Green, or standard
Sapphire Grey! As little as $1.25
a week buys any model.

SMITH-CORONA INC SYRACUSE 1 N.Y. FACTORIES ALSO IN TORONTO, BRUSSELS AND JOHANNESBURG

Previous, left: Print advertisement for Olivetti, December 1957. Reproduced with permission from Olivetti S.p.A.

Previous, center: Print advertisement for IBM, 1960s. Reprint Courtesy of International Business Machines Corporation, © International Business Machines Corporation.

Previous, right: Print advertisement for Smith-Corona, November, 1955. Reproduced with permission from Smith-Corona.

Right: *House Beautiful*, December 1963. Reprinted with permission of Hearst Communications, Inc.

This new self-dialing phone is a wonderful convenience for people working without a secretary—the busy executive or housewife. Numbers frequently called are punched in code on plastic cards. With a card in the slot, you press the start bar and the number is dialed automatically. Card-dialer phone, about $3.50 monthly plus installation charges; available from your local telephone company.

Gifts you couldn't give before

● Here are 16 of the most exciting gifts of the year. Why? Because most of them were still on the drawing board at this time last year, so very few people even know about them. Each is designed to perform a specific function useful in contemporary life. The prices range from a few pennies to hundreds of dollars, so your choice is wide. All are practical, useful gifts, perfect presentations for those on your list who seem to have everything.

The know-how of an expert carver is built into this electric knife. By merely pressing the control switch and guiding the knife, its reciprocating blades cut neat, uniform slices, thick

He will have the world at his fingertips with this small three-band portable radio. It receives international short wave, weather alerts, and marine broadcasts, as well as standard AM

Advertisement for Reynolds Metals foil gift wraps, 1960s. Reproduced with permission from Reynolds Consumer Products.

Gifts & Greetings

CHAPTER FOUR

Christmas Is in Your Hands

Christmas and craft go hand in hand. I made more than my share of holiday decorations as a kid and even dabbled in making origami ornaments during bouts of procrastination in college and grad school. Homemade and handmade are sometimes the ugly ducklings of Christmas gifts, but however they look, it's hard not to be moved that someone would spend the time and energy to create something unique for someone else, when simply buying something has never been easier.

And, indeed, we tend to think of the postwar boom years as a golden age for corporations, bolstered as they were by the dawn of television, supermarkets, and shopping malls. This was true, but it wasn't necessarily a dry spell for the home-made or the handcrafted, either. The industrial sheen of the era can play

Right: Originally published in *Better Homes and Gardens*® magazine, December 1956.

Opposite: *House Beautiful*, December 1963. Reprinted with permission of Hearst Communications, Inc.

tricks on the eye, with its gigantic cars and pale-pink appliances distracting our attention from the vibrant studio craft movement that was taking root in America—the fruits of which are more popular than ever at today's high-end design auctions and in the pages of West Elm or Design Within Reach catalogs. Even more widespread was an early incarnation of the DIY movement, which fused the ingenuity of wartime austerity with the material abundance of the 1950s and '60s. Food and craft project ideas were major features of magazine spreads, crystallizing the American homemaker's position as a domestic creative force whose raw materials were glossy and heavily advertised.

Shelf-stable, canned, Technicolor postwar food embodies everything we've been taught to reject by Michael Pollan and the farm-to-table movement of the early twenty-first century. But viewed in the context of World War II itself, the midcentury obsession with convenience foods makes a certain amount of sense. Shelf-stable food as we know it today was a wartime innovation that was adapted, like so many other inventions, for civilian use. A suburban homemaker who preferred not to have to visit the grocery store every day could stock up on frozen and canned goods instead, secure in the knowledge that her purchases would not be wasted. For a generation that remembered the Great Depression and wartime rationing, this was real progress, and in the 1950s no one worried much about artificial flavors and colors or whether preservatives were safe.

Christmas foods were no different, and just as companies like Reynolds Metals, DuPont, and 3M taught consumers how to use aluminum foil, cellophane, and tape to create festive holiday decorations, food companies like Pillsbury and Nestlé thought up new ways to bake, cook, and serve holiday treats using off-the-shelf ingredients.

When rationing severely limited the materials available for decoration during World War II, magazines and hobby craft pamphlets offered do-it-yourself ideas that creative families could try at relatively little expense, often using seasonally appropriate materials like pinecones or evergreen branches. The postwar boom initiated a period of unprecedented material abundance, making supplies easy to come by. But that DIY ethos never really went away—it just got shinier. Companies saw branding and sales opportunities in the rising popularity of DIY projects as hobbies for both kids and adults, and the world of Christmas crafting was an ideal platform to demonstrate a particular material's unexpected festive uses.

Left: *House Beautiful*, December 1961. Reprinted with permission of Hearst Communications, Inc.

Right: Star Bright fabric Christmas tree, 1950s. Photo by Jeffrey Stockbridge.

The Craft of Christmas

Beginning in 1939, a constellation of craft groups led by philanthropist Aileen Osborn Webb formed the Handcraft Cooperative League of America, which would later coalesce into the American Craft Council. Webb came from a family of art collectors, and her brother, General Frederick Osborn, established the Army Arts and Crafts Program, which provided an early form of what we now call art therapy, and encouraged some returning veterans to further their art education under the G.I. Bill. Webb believed in craft's ability to change lives, elevate and refine public taste, and connect present-day America to its preindustrial heritage in a tangible way. She established America House, a retail outlet for contemporary fine craft, in New York City in 1940; the School for American Crafts, which is now part of RIT in Rochester, New York; and the Museum of Contemporary Crafts, now known as the Museum of Arts and Design, in 1956. The early newsletter of the Handcraft Cooperative League would evolve into a magazine called *Craft*

Alexander Girard, carved wooden Nativity scene, 1953. Image © 2016 Girard Studio, LLC. All rights reserved.

Horizons in 1941, and throughout the 1950s and early '60s, it was a treasure trove of photography, illustration, and critical writing on craft, both in the West and around the world. The vogue for Scandinavian folk art, Japanese pottery, South American textiles, handwrought metal jewelry, and scores of other global treasures were featured in *Craft Horizons* right before they would appear in the pages of *House Beautiful* or *Better Homes and Gardens*. At Christmastime, *Craft Horizons* would feature gift and decorating ideas for a readership that was on the bohemian end of the American design spectrum.

Folk art and the handmade had a surprising degree of resonance for many giants of midcentury design. Its influence offered a cozy and colorful counterweight to the sleek and sometimes chilly aesthetic of modernism. Charles and Ray Eames collected figurines, toys, and textiles from their international travels, as did the prolific designer Alexander Girard (1907–93), who created an array of vibrant textile designs for the Herman Miller Company, many of which are still in production today. His textiles were used to upholster the furniture of George Nelson and Charles and Ray

Craft Horizons, "Christmas Shopper," December 1960.
Courtesy American Craft Council.

Craft Horizons,
December 1952
Courtesy American
Craft Council.

Craft Horizons, "Christmas Shopper of American Crafts," December 1965.
Courtesy American Craft Council.

Eames, and he gained wide acclaim in the mid-1960s for his rebranding, with the offices of the advertising agency Wells Rich Greene, of Braniff International Airways. For the Braniff project, which used the tagline "The End of the Plain Plane," he designed a bold graphic identity and a suite of color-saturated fabrics that complemented far-out flight attendant uniforms by Emilio Pucci and aircraft that were painted in psychedelic colors. Girard and his wife Susan were enthusiastic collectors of folk art from around the world, especially dolls and toys from South America; part of their collection is now housed at Santa Fe's Museum of International Folk Art. In 1962 Girard organized an exhibition called "The Nativity" at the Nelson Gallery of Art (now the Nelson-Atkins Museum of Art) in Kansas City, Missouri, which was supported in part by Hallmark Cards. The exhibition features more than 150 Nativity sets from Girard's collection, mainly from Europe and South America. The vibrant exhibition poster itself has become a collector's item. Girard designed a Nativity set of his own on the occasion of the exhibition, which featured brightly colored, two-dimensional wooden figures that were at once ancient-seeming and ultra-mod thanks to their simple, geometric shapes, charming style, and bold hues.

Alexander Girard, manger print, 1960s. Image © 2016 Girard Studio, LLC. All rights reserved.

Midcentury Christmas

Alexander Girard, poster for "The Nativity" at the Nelson Gallery of Art, 1962.
Image © 2016 Girard Studio, LLC. All rights reserved.

Christmas Is in Your Hands

a hearthside supper for your tree-trimmers

By GRACE WHITE

Say "Merry Christmas!" with...

IT's Christmas all through the house—garlands of greenery at the door, gala decor in every room, heavenly aromas in the kitchen. On these 10 pages we give you merry-Christmas ideas aplenty— with recipes and how-to instructions for all. Here, the fun of trimming the tree and a warming hearthside supper start the family's festive season

Recipes begin on page 66. Instructions for making the decorations start on page 75

see **b**uyer's **g**uide

Santa's helpers ready to eat? Give them big mugfuls of hearty **Minute Minestrone** (a mix makes it speedy) with toasty buns; **Golden Oyster Scallop** decked with a parsley wreath; relishes; and the creamiest of holiday delights—**Eggnog Trifle**

Do-It-Yourself, Inc.

The December 1958 issue of Family Circle magazine contained how-to articles about making personalized felt stockings for each child in the family, as well as instructions for making "indestructible" Christmas ornaments out of paper doilies, pipe cleaners, glitter, glue, and ribbon, all products available at "variety stores." Amy Vanderbilt provided etiquette tips for how Christmas cards should be formatted, addressed, and printed (preferably signed by hand). A colorful spread picturing a family trimming their tree in front of an ultramodern white brick fireplace offered ideas for finger foods to serve during decorating parties, each image including a handcrafted piece of holiday decor alongside stylish displays of food and drink.

The pages of *Better Homes and Gardens* were full of interior design ideas year-round and tended to focus more on interior

Originally published in *Family Circle*® magazine, December 1958.

glamour than family time. Nevertheless, the pages of *Better Homes* were full of festive ideas, including gifts for men that encouraged handyman tendencies, like power tools that could help outfit a "home workshop," though the tackling of actual needed repairs is rarely mentioned. An article called "Decorate with Nature's Gifts" in the December 1956 issue shows—at the height of the Cold War consumer boom—how families could create Nativity scenes, ornaments, and holiday decorations for their homes using everyday found objects like branches, dried seed pods, shells, and even live moss. The clear influence of folk art and the studio craft movement is evident in the images of project ideas like the "winter miniature," comprised of a piece of driftwood with evergreen branches, or the natural centerpiece that resembles a Japanese bonsai tree. The rustic aesthetic of the craft scene is fused here with the colorful sheen of the mass marketplace, yielding a curious and compelling result, part Space Age and part hippie macramé. And, perhaps knowingly referring back to the old practice of decorating with real fruit, this article suggests using shiny red apples and holly sprigs to welcome guests by the front door.

Originally published in *Better Homes and Gardens*® magazine, December 1956.

Originally published in *Better Homes and Gardens®*
magazine, December 1956.

Originally published in the *Better Homes and Gardens Treasury of Christmas Ideas*, 1966.

Midcentury Christmas

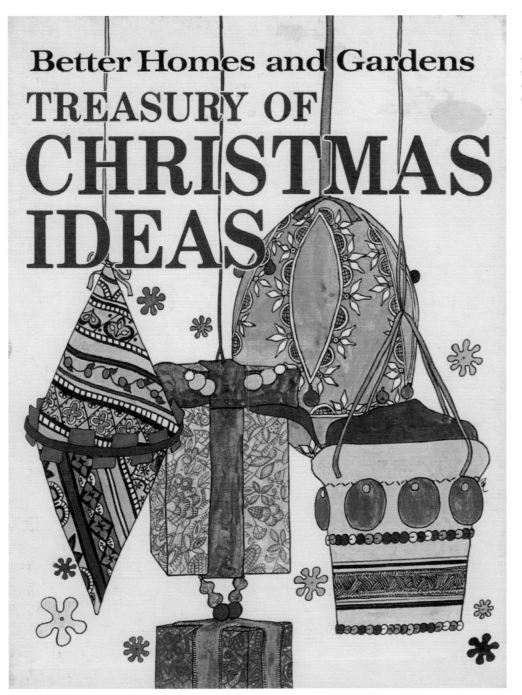

Better Homes and Gardens
TREASURY OF CHRISTMAS IDEAS

Originally published in
the *Better Homes and
Gardens Treasury of
Christmas Ideas*, 1966.

MOLDING

FORMING CONE

COVERING

BASIC METHODS FOR WORKING WITH FOIL

Aluminum foil makes it easy to create special decorations in your home. Here are some of the basic techniques devised for working with the versatile material:

PLEATING Accordion-pleated aluminum foil is needed for several of the designs in this book. It is simple to do and makes the foil stronger for forming large figures. To pleat, tear a sheet of foil of the desired length from the roll. Lay the sheet on a flat surface and fold over about an inch of the foil, beginning at one lengthwise edge of the foil. Now, double this folded portion back against the foil sheet, creasing foil to form another fold. Repeat this process, folding back and forth, until entire sheet is pleated.

CRUSHING Crushed foil can be used to make wreaths, letters, small animals, and many other ideas given in this book. Crushing is the basic operation for making the large animals in Conny's Zoo. Beginning with a sheet of foil, crush lightly with the hands along the lengthwise direction. This light crushing can result in circles of foil for various decorations, long ropes of foil, or narrow foil for forming letters.

COVERING Ordinary drinking straws covered with aluminum foil can make delightful mobiles and table decorations when combined with artificial flowers or nuts. A piece of aluminum foil about 2 inches long will cover a straw. Simply lay the foil on a flat surface, place straw on top of long edge, and roll straw, taking foil along with it. A group of these foil-covered straws, tied or wired together at the center, can be formed into a lovely starburst effect. Boxes of all types can be covered with aluminum foil. Cover top and bottom separately for smooth appearance and reusability of the gift container. Designs of colored tape, construction paper, poster paint can be used to "dress up" an ordinary box covered with foil.

MOLDING An almost unending number of shapes can be created by molding several layers of aluminum foil over an object of desired form. When removed, the foil retains the shape of the object. This technique will produce a bell by shaping Alcoa Wrap over a custard cup or bell-shaped glass. A reflector star can be molded using a common star-shaped candle holder.

FORMING CONE Cones are used in many of the designs in this book. They are easy to make and can be made of any desired size. Cut a circle of foil or paper and make a cut with scissors into the center. Now, form circle into a cone and hold with cellophane tape or glue.

Instructions from *Alcoa's Book of Decorations* by Conny von Hagen, Golden Press, 1959.
Reproduced with permission from Alcoa, Inc.

Christmas Is in Your Hands

it's a container, a gift wrap, a centerpiece . . .
Just mold five Alcoa Wrap sheets over an inverted bowl. Cut off excess
foil, leaving an even one-in. rim. Remove bowl. Repeat procedure to make
top half; then crush a sheet of foil into a ball and place on top. Add
two more foil sheets to hold head and top of body together. Remove bowl
and cut rim. For the hat, cover a paper cup with felt, cut a brim. Use black
buttons for coat and eyes, and a red one for the nose. The broom is
a red paper fringe with a crushed foil stick.

cover photo—woven stars
Cut 2 in. strips of Alcoa Wrap, place
straw on long edge and add a bit
of white glue, then roll straw in foil.
Cover four straws. Cross them in
center. Hold straws and weave a
ribbon in and out, as much as you
like. Glue ribbon end to fasten.
Cut straw ends to points and
hang on a thin thread.

Instructions for crafting an aluminum snowman and table decorations, Alcoa Aluminum Newsletter, December 1967. Aluminum Company
of America Records, 1857-1992 (bulk 1900-65), MSS 282, Detre Library & Archives, Sen. John Heinz History Center.

Midcentury Christmas

molded angel
To make this little angel your own, place a wad of foil on top of an inverted tumbler and crush three Alcoa Wrap sheets over it. Cut excess foil, leaving a narrow rim. Remove tumbler. For the face, cut a pink felt or paper circle, glue in place, then add eyelashes, a little red nose and a foil halo. Artificial flowers are pinned or glued around top half of face. The wings are cut from construction paper and taped to back.

mexican church
Use a medium size box. Cut away all but three sides. Mark and cut out towers, roof line and doors. Cover entire box with Alcoa Wrap. Cut out window frames, crosses, door and roof decorations from brightly colored paper and glue into place. Fasten small bells in each tower. Tape sides of box together to make a triangle. Fill with graceful candles and listen—you might hear the bells ring!

Instructions for crafting an aluminum snowman and table decorations, Alcoa Aluminum Newsletter, December 1967. Aluminum Company of America Records, 1857–1992 (bulk 1900–65), MSS 282, Detre Library & Archives, Sen. John Heinz History Center.

Christmas Is in Your Hands

In the same issue, which contains
print ads from both Reynolds Metals and
Alcoa, advertising both aluminum kitchenware
as holiday gifts and plain aluminum foil as a holiday
decorating material, an article titled "Make these Dazzlers
from Foil Plates" illustrates a project for kids using aluminum
pie tins to create two- and three-dimensional displays. Pie tins
can be stamped, crimped, painted, and decorated with glue and
glitter to create unique Christmas ornaments and over-
mantel displays, even shiny wreaths.
The December 1958 special issue,
devoted entirely to holiday ideas, features elaborate
decorating projects ranging from Japanese-inspired
DIY Christmas trees to tropical-themed parties
complete with colorful fishing nets
and palm fronds.

The 1959 *Alcoa's Book of Decorations* by Conny von Hagen is a treasury of design ideas that includes projects for Christmas, Easter, birthdays, and all sorts of other occasions. The Christmas section is the largest, and its subtitle says it all: "Christmas Is in Your Hands." Projects illustrated here include handmade baskets for stashing sweets created from the branches of a Christmas tree (echoing a very old European custom), foil stockings for the fireplace, foil accessories like Santa Claus's belt buckle and boots, foil angels (cone-shaped and relatively easy to make), and foil wreaths for the front door.

An article in the same issue on how to make trees from scratch dispenses with the idea of creating ornaments in favor of building a faux tree out of paper, foil, candy canes, and even yarn and cardboard, along with handcrafted paper cards and decorated gifts that look "too pretty to open." The *Better Homes and Gardens Treasury of Christmas Ideas*, a book published in 1966,

contained scores of ideas with an even craftier bent, appearing as it did once the fiber art craze of the '60s and '70s was well underway. Ideas for festive wall hangings woven from yarn or made from felt feature bright colors and abstract designs, while Christmas card ideas feature the techniques of stitching and knotting alongside folding and cutting paper for graphic effect. A loom is suggested as an ideal gift for a teenage girl.

3M produced similar glossy guides in the late 1950s—they were circulated with issues of *American Home* and *McCall's* magazines. The 3M brands of Scotch tape and Sasheen ribbon are put to graphic use as though they were paints and brushes, with colorful stripes and bands running across walls, windows, presents, trees, tablescapes, cards, and of course, under the tree. An elegant DIY "stained-glass window" made with colorful cellophane and Scotch tape gives a modernist house with a big picture window a touch of faux-Gothic charm. Gifts are customized using tape to spell out names or "draw" the

Above and opposite: Originally published in the *Better Homes and Gardens Treasury of Christmas Ideas*, 1966.

Stoles above were knit on a hand-made loom. Loom measures 3¾ x 27½ inches and stands 4¼ inches tall. An uneven number (45) of No. 16 wire brads are spaced ½ inch apart across the loom with ½ inch distance between parallel nails. Brads also extend ½ inch above surface of loom. To thread, use methods A or B below, running the yarn over every other nail one way, then back over empty ones. Repeat process so there are two threads around each nail.

To knit, take up bottom thread with crochet hook. Pull loop over thread above it, drop on other side of nail. Repeat step at each nail. Each nail now has one thread. Set up threading pattern again. Add one row

to get stacked effect. Knit off bottom threads as before. Continue until stole is as long as desired. Beginning on loom right, pick up end stitch on one rail, drop over corresponding nail on opposite rail. Take lower thread, lift over upper thread and nail as in knitting. Repeat for each pair of nails. Begin again at right, take loop off first nail, drop next. Knit off one thread. Take remaining loop off nail, drop over third nail. Continue to last stitch, fasten as in regular knitting.

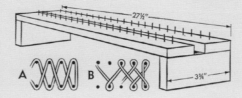

CHRISTMAS MAGIC

FOR ALL YOUR GIFTS

USING "SCOTCH" BRAND TAPES AND "SASHEEN" BRAND RIBBON

"Christmas Magic" gift-wrapping guide, Scotch Brand Tapes, 3M Company, ca. 1965. Used with permission.

A potpourri of tips for home and gifts

◀ **WEATHERPROOF YOUR MAILING LABELS.** Smart and simple trick when mailing gifts. Protect addresses from ink-smearing snow or rain; cover them completely with "Scotch" brand Cellophane Tape to help assure safe arrivals.

◀ **GIFT TAGS.** A great new idea! "Scotch" brand Gift Tapes you can write on—plus bright stickers, 40 on a roll. Just snip them off and press down for new labeling speed and ease.

◀ **IDENTIFY GIFT GIVERS.** End "thank you" note mix-ups. Keep "Scotch" Cellophane Tape at hand during the bustle of opening gifts; use it to attach givers' names to packages (or to gifts) as they're opened.

◀ **STOCKING STUFFER.** Drop several rolls of "Scotch" Cellophane Tape . . . or left-over rolls of Gift Tape . . . in the youngsters' Christmas stockings. Just watch them put the tape to creative use during many play time hours.

Midcentury Christmas

COVER PACKAGES:

Front row, left to right: Tree Tapecraft. Gift tape makes tree design. *Glitter Magic.* Make Glitter Wands (see "Friendship House" page). Fasten with a long loop of tape, sticky side out; press flat. Sprinkle with glitter. *Christmas Carnation.* Make "Magic Bow". Crush together loops, snip off ends (b). *Glitter Bow.* Make as in Dazzle Wreath. Spell out names with gay gift tape. *Name Dropper. Back row, left to right: Bow Magic.* Make a large "Magic Bow". *Harum-Scarum.* Even left-over ends of gift tape look glamorous here. *Holly Bait.* Add sprigs of holly (or pine) using "SCOTCH" Cellophane Tape.

◄ **DAZZLE WREATH.** Front-door dress-up with Glitter Bows (or any "SASHEEN" bow). Make "Magic Bows". Then press loop ends together (a) and cut V-notches in as many loops as you like. Back cutouts with "SCOTCH" Cellophane Tape and sprinkle with glitter. Form a wire coat hanger into a circle and tape or tie on bows.

◄ **CHRISTMAS STORY ON TAPE.** The holiday classic, "'Twas the Night Before Christmas", re-told and pictured on a roll of "SCOTCH" Gift Tape. Fun to tell from start to finish on children's gift wraps or Christmas cards.

◄ **CENTERPIECE CAKE.** Focal point of your festive holiday table . . . this gay cake with Fluffy White Frosting. Make 2 "Magic Bows" of "SASHEEN". Tie a bow to each side of a cluster of four candy canes; tuck in center of cake. Dot sides with crumbled candy cane.

WRITE IN for the "how-to" of creating flower bows the "Magic Bow" way. From daisies to dahlias, these "SASHEEN" bows rate raves with little extra effort—glamorize gifts. Send to Dept. GBC-129, 3M Co., St. Paul 6, Minnesota.

"SCOTCH", "SASHEEN", "DECORETTE" and "MAGIC BOW" are registered trademarks of 3M Co., St. Paul 6, Minn. Export: 99 Park Ave., N.Y. Canada: London, Ontario. "Magic Bow" and method of making patented U.S. Pat. No. RE23035.

MINNESOTA MINING AND MANUFACTURING COMPANY
. . . WHERE RESEARCH IS THE KEY TO TOMORROW

3M COMPANY

Christmas Is in Your Hands

Best Loved Foods of Christmas

for the most wonderful time of all—when only the BEST will do

BEST *of the* **BAKE-OFF**

65 Recipes for America's hospitable holiday season featuring the 10 BEST Butter Cookies

25¢

Chocolate Pinwheels

Developed by Ann Pillsbury

BAKE at 375° for 7 to 10 minutes.   MAKES about 4 dozen cookies.

Sift together...	1¾ cups sifted **Pillsbury's Best All Purpose Flour***
	½ teaspoon double-acting **baking powder**
	¼ teaspoon **salt**
Cream........	½ cup **butter.** Gradually add
	½ cup **sugar,** creaming well.
Blend in.......	1 unbeaten **egg** and
	1 teaspoon **French's Vanilla.** Beat well.
Add..........	the dry ingredients gradually; mix thoroughly.
Place.........	half of dough on waxed paper. Blend
	1 square (1 oz.) melted unsweetened **chocolate** into remaining dough. Chill doughs for easier handling, about 1 hour.
Roll out.......	light dough on floured waxed paper to a 15x7-inch rectangle. Repeat with chocolate dough. Place chocolate dough on top of light dough. Roll as for jelly roll starting with 15-inch side. Wrap in waxed paper. Chill at least 2 hours.
Cut..........	into ¼-inch slices; place on ungreased baking sheets.
Bake.........	in moderate oven (375°) 7 to 10 minutes until delicately browned.

**For use with Pillsbury's Best Self-Rising Flour, omit baking powder and salt.*

"Best Loved Foods of Christmas," ca. 1965.
Used with permission of General Mills Marketing, Inc. (GMMI).

silhouette of a Christmas tree. Wreaths are fashioned from red ribbon, and fluffy white cakes are topped with ribbon flowers.

If baked goods festooned with inedible flourishes were perhaps more appealing in photographs than in reality, plenty of major food companies produced practical guides for holiday entertaining, with baking a particular favorite. Pillsbury, which continues to hold its famed Bake-Off competition to this day, produced a booklet in the early 1960s called "Best Loved Foods of Christmas" that was so extensive it had its own index.

The recipes included many by Ann Pillsbury herself, as well as winning recipes from previous Bake-Off contestants, all organized by type (bar cookies, cakes, frostings, and so on). The booklet is illustrated with cheery, faintly mod drawings of Santa Claus, several helpful angels, and a family enjoying fresh-baked creations like Chocolate Pinwheels, which Santa is shown serving on a platter. Like the Alcoa and Scotch guides, the Pillsbury baking guide was aimed at homemakers who wanted to manifest a traditional kind of Christmas coziness, but were also in search of new ideas and novel recipes to make an impression on guests and set their culinary creations apart. In this respect, it perfectly illustrates the fusion of the inventive DIY spirit of the craft world with the glossy visual landscape of television and magazines.

Christmas Recipes

Consumers Power Company 1969

Glamor Desserts

CHRISTMAS RECIPES

CONSUMERS POWER 1970

"Christmas Recipes," Consumers Power Company, 1970. Reproduced with permission from Consumer's Energy.

Opposite, left: "Christmas Recipes," Consumers Power Company, 1969. Reproduced with permission from Consumer's Energy.

Opposite, right: Illustrations by Ruth McCrea, from *The Merrie Christmas Cook Book*. Published in 1955 by Peter Pauper Press, Inc. www.peterpauper.com. Used by permission.

TREASURY OF CHRISTMAS IDEAS

HOLIDAY RECIPES   THINGS TO MAKE   LIGHT-TIME DECORATING   GIFT IDEAS

"Treasury of Christmas Ideas" Western Light and Telephone Company Home Services Department, 1960s.
Reproduced with permission from Energy Future Holdings/TXU Energy.

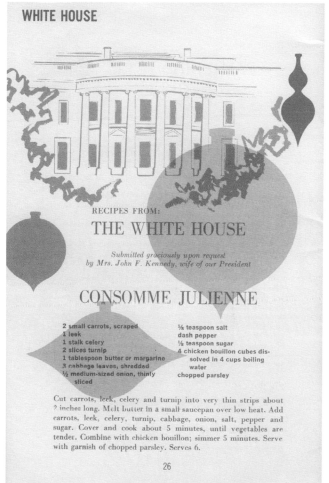

WHITE HOUSE

RECIPES FROM:

THE WHITE HOUSE

Submitted graciously upon request
by Mrs. John F. Kennedy, wife of our President

CONSOMME JULIENNE

2 small carrots, scraped
1 leek
1 stalk celery
2 slices turnip
1 tablespoon butter or margarine
3 cabbage leaves, shredded
½ medium-sized onion, thinly
   sliced

⅛ teaspoon salt
dash pepper
⅛ teaspoon sugar
4 chicken bouillon cubes dis-
   solved in 4 cups boiling
   water
chopped parsley

Cut carrots, leek, celery and turnip into very thin strips about
2 inches long. Melt butter in a small saucepan over low heat. Add
carrots, leek, celery, turnip, cabbage, onion, salt, pepper and
sugar. Cover and cook about 5 minutes, until vegetables are
tender. Combine with chicken bouillon; simmer 5 minutes. Serve
with garnish of chopped parsley. Serves 6.

26

"A Christmas Cookbook of Many Lands," Rehabilitation Center of Greater St. Louis, ca. 1961–62.
Reproduced with permission from Laclede Gas Company.

Gift-Wrapping

IT'S WHAT'S in the gift package that counts, to be sure, but there's no getting away from it—the wrapping creates the first impression. Nothing will take the edge off lively anticipation so much as a messy, hard-to-undo package.

The first step in thoughtful holiday gift wrapping lies in the correct selection of paper and ribbon. The size and shape of the package and the taste of the recipient should be carefully considered. Large patterns are available for large packages, small designs for the little parcels. Frequently a part of a large pattern is perfect for a spe-

cific small pac[...]
is to center th[...]
of the packag[...]
the design is [...]
then be place[...]
does not cov[...]
desired effect.[...]
are especially[...]
over repeat pa[...]
anywhere, bu[...]
left to show,[...]
Appropriate [...]
should be se[...]
taste, whether[...]

MAGIC

All that is required then
[pap]er properly on the face
just the desired part of
[wei]ghted. The bow should
the package so that it
[th]e design and ruin the
[?]onal patterns and stripes
[?] for round boxes. All-
[?]s allow for a bow almost
[?]orial designs should be
[?] a bow off to one side.
[?]ns in wrapping paper
[?] to suit the recipient's
[?] masculine or feminine,

Afterword

A *Charlie Brown Christmas* first aired on CBS on December 9, 1965, with its indelible, jazz-inflected piano soundtrack by Vince Guaraldi and perhaps the most famous aluminum Christmas tree of all time playing a starring role. In the five decades since, it's safe to say that aluminum trees have never quite returned to such prominence, but the postwar aesthetic and modernism itself have never been more popular. Yet we don't know quite what to make of this time period; the cool chairs, Sputnik chandeliers, and graphic design we love today furnished a society that didn't give women or Americans of color their full civil rights. It gave rise to both the space race and the arms race. What *A Charlie Brown Christmas* captures so beautifully, and perhaps why it's still so well-loved, is that our feelings about shopping, feasting, decorating, and, indeed, Christmas itself are complicated, and always (at least since about 1830) reflect our fraught relationship with consumer culture. That Charlie Brown chose a beat-up, sad-looking little tree at the height of American Cold War prosperity—and that we cheer his good

Popular Mechanics Christmas Handbook, 1952. Reprinted with permission of Hearst Communications, Inc.

taste—speaks to the DIY, inventive crafter in all of us. That spirit shaped the look and feel of midcentury Christmas in all kinds of ways that make perfect sense given the holiday's long history as a time of year for trying new things and cultivating a sense of wonder for young and old. Some chose to do so by harnessing the abundance and new materials of the era, while others dusted off their wartime grit by making their own festive fun with simple materials. Still others, like Theodor Geisel (aka Dr. Seuss) and Charles Schulz (creator of Peanuts), created lovable characters who ask us to take a good look at the miracles of love and friendship that surround us all the time, and celebrate that on Christmas, tree or no tree.

Today, in the era of the Buy Nothing Christmas, our purchases are linked to something that Cold War Americans didn't worry much about: our carbon footprint. We talk now about focusing on experiences rather than things. And in a sense, we have the postwar era to thank for this point of view, though all the shiny lights and new appliances might distract us. If there was one thing Americans knew how to do well in the 1950s and '60s, it was nesting and making the most of being at home. Sure, it didn't hurt that teenagers had their own Princess telephones

Popular Mechanics Christmas Handbook, 1952.
Reprinted with permission of Hearst Communications, Inc.

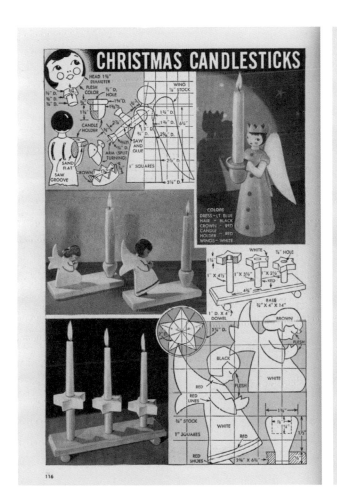

Popular Mechanics Christmas Handbook, 1952.
Reprinted with permission of Hearst Communications, Inc.

Afterword

227

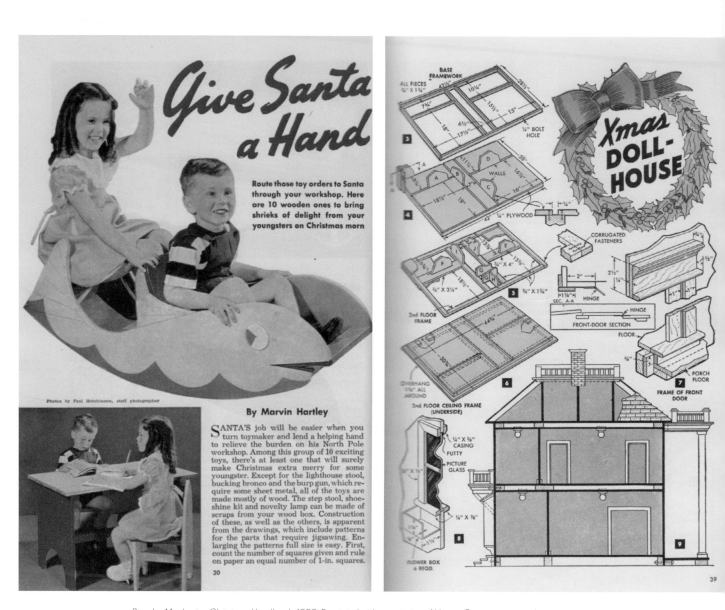

Popular Mechanics Christmas Handbook, 1952. Reprinted with permission of Hearst Communications, Inc.

and younger siblings could watch Bonanza on TV, all without leaving the house. But the focus on domestic life, playing games, baking, entertaining, decorating the tree, and undertaking perhaps ill-advised but nevertheless fun craft projects is exactly the kind of family-focused Christmas that the early Victorians imagined when austere St. Nicholas underwent his transformation into jolly Santa Claus.

At one poignant moment in A Charlie Brown Christmas, a forlorn Charlie Brown asks Linus what Christmas is all about, and—totally without irony—Linus recites the text of the Annunciation to the Shepherds from Luke 2:8–14. The last line is: "Glory to God in the highest, and on Earth peace, and goodwill toward men," which, according to Linus, is what Christmas is all about. Cold War Americans knew a thing or two about the wish for peace on Earth; after surviving two world wars and an economic depression, faced with the threat of yet another (far scarier) war with nuclear potential, their response was to cherish those close to home. Since the days before Yule and Saturnalia evolved into Christmas as we know it, the holidays of midwinter have been about enjoying time together and celebrating a job well done, whether it's final exams, the end of harvest season, or wrapping up a big project at the office. The look of the more commercial side of the postwar era may be a bit shiny and glossy for our artisanal tastes nowadays, but the inventiveness and creativity with which they celebrated together is still inspiring.

If you tire of shopping, and the spirit of the Buy Nothing movement inspires you, skip Black Friday, and take a cue from the craft experts of the 1950s to festoon your home with DIY holiday splendor. Or, better yet, pack up your supplies and spend time helping someone else who needs a dose of holiday cheer and some good, crafty company. Linus, Charlie Brown, and even Lucy would agree: That is what Christmas is all about.

Alexander Girard, *International Love Heart*, 1966. Image © 2016 Girard Studio, LLC. All rights reserved.

ACKNOWLEDGMENTS

This book is a celebration of holiday cheer and postwar optimism, and I would not have been able to complete it nearly as cheerfully without the unflagging support and inspiration of numerous important elves, chief among them my wonderful agent Leslie Stoker, my endlessly patient and creative editor Ann Treistman, researcher extraordinaire Peggy Ann Brown, publicity maven Devorah Backman, and designer LeAnna Weller Smith. I'm indebted to the librarians, archivists, and curators across the country for their help unearthing objects and information, especially Yen H. Wu and Regan Brumagen at the Corning Museum of Glass, Anne-Marie Jacobus at Corning, Inc., lighting expert Jeff Carter, Matthew Strauss at the Heinz History Center, Victoria Gray at the Strong National Museum of Play, Jennifer Belt at Art Resource, researcher Kris Lipkowski, and the staff of the Chicago History Museum.

The descendants and friends of the legendary designers whose work is featured here were generous with their time and expertise, especially Eliza Brownjohn, Aleishall Girard Maxon, Russell Flinchum and Gail Dreyfuss Wilson, Eames Demetrios, Genevieve Fong, and David Hertsgaard of the Eames Office, as well as Lesley Whitworth of the University of Brighton Design Archives. Numerous companies were kind enough to grant me permission to reproduce vintage treasures, and I'm especially grateful to Mary Ann Milo of GE Lighting, Natalie Peters of Pillsbury, Joyce Saltzman of Alcoa, and Kris Hildy of Reynolds. My friends in the design history world provided invaluable inspiration and encouragement, particularly Glenn Adamson, Luke Baker, Elizabeth Essner, Alexandra Lange, Sarah Lichtman, and Amy Snyder. The team at KB Park, particularly Jared Seeger, Justin Kitrosser, and Alex Cave gave me the flexibility I needed to complete this project and lots of good cheer along the way.

Midcentury Christmas is dedicated to my mother, Kathy Blaney-Miller, whose special holiday inventiveness and inspiring passion for cultural history sparkle from the pages of this book. My stepfather, Peter Miller, and uncle, John Blaney, have made every Christmas the kind of kinetic wonderland that an only child can only dream of, and they each continue to inspire me. My future in-laws, Meryl and Chaim Citron, have been supportive and delightfully curious about my research. Last but not least, my fiancé, Manny Citron, has cheered me on from the earliest incarnations of the proposal that led to this book, offering sage advice, perspective, support, dinners, and love at every turn. I could not have written this book without him.

Originally published in *Better Homes and Gardens*® magazine, December 1958.

SOURCES

Akers, Kevin. *All Wrapped Up!: Groovy Gift Wrap of the 1960s*. San Francisco: Chronicle Books, 2005.

American Christmas Cards 1900–1960. Edited by Kenneth L. Ames. New York: Bard Graduate Center, 2011.

Bird, William L. *Holidays on Display*. Princeton, NJ: Princeton Architectural Press, 2007.

Brunner, Bernd. *Inventing the Christmas Tree*. New Haven, CT: Yale University Press, 2012.

Lindemann, J. and J. Shimon. *Season's Gleamings: The Art of the Aluminum Christmas Tree*. New York: Melcher Media, 2004.

Marling, Karal Ann. *Merry Christmas!: Celebrating America's Greatest Holiday*. Cambridge, MA: Harvard University Press, 2009.

May, Elaine Tyler. *Homeward Bound: American Families in the Cold War Era*. New York: Basic Books, 2008.

Mozingo, Louise A. *Pastoral Capitalism: A History of Suburban Corporate Landscapes*. Cambridge, MA: MIT Press, 2011.

Nissenbaum, Stephen. *The Battle for Christmas*. New York: Vintage, 1997.

Savig, Mary and Faythe Levine. *Handmade Holiday Cards from 20th-Century Artists*. Washington, DC: Smithsonian Books, 2012.

Schmidt, Leigh Eric. *Consumer Rites: The Buying and Selling of American Holidays*. Princeton, NJ: Princeton University Press, 1997.

Sheller, Mimi. *Aluminum Dreams: The Making of Light Modernity*. Cambridge, MA: MIT Press, 2014.

Waits, William. *The Modern Christmas in America: A Cultural History of Gift Giving*. New York: NYU Press, 1994.